Praise for A. C. Grayling

'[Grayling] is not afraid to engage with his fellows and their times. He avoids needless technicality and is prepared to allow that non-philosophers are capable of engaging with the issues at hand. Add to that an elegance of style, a sense of humour and the ability to juxtapose serious musings with wild and wacky facts ... and you have an easily digestible form of philosophy'
Fiona Ellis, *TLS*

'Here is an author who is certainly not cowed by large subjects ... There is much fine, delicious writing here'
Noel Malcolm, *Sunday Telegraph*

'This enlightened and enlightening task ... the whole thing is delightfully brainy'   *Private Eye*

'Shows how much understanding people can gain about themselves and their world by reflecting on the lessons learned by science, the arts and history'   *Irish Examiner* (Cork)

'Grayling is a careful arbitrator of the great philosophers' arguments. On the ancient sites of their wisdom, his own insights and consolations sparkle like bright new stones'
Belinda McKeon, *Irish Times*

A. C. Grayling is Professor of Philosophy at Birkbeck College, University of London, and a Supernumerary Fellow of St Anne's College, Oxford. He is the author of numerous books, and is also a distinguished literary journalist and broadcaster. He has been a columnist for the *Guardian* and *The Times*, is a Contributing Editor of *Prospect* magazine, and Editor of Online Review London. He is a Fellow of both the Royal Society of Literature and the Royal Society of Arts. His website can be visited at www.acgrayling.com.

By A. C. Grayling

The Refutation of Scepticism
Berkeley: The Central Arguments
The Long March to the Fourth of June (*as Li Xiao Jun*)
Wittgenstein
China: A Literary Companion (*with S. Whitfield*)
Moral Values
An Introduction to Philosophical Logic
Russell
The Quarrel of the Age: The Life and Times of William Hazlitt
The Meaning of Things
The Reason of Things
What is Good?: The Search for the Best Way to Live
The Mystery of Things
The Heart of Things
Descartes
The Form of Things
In Freedom's Name
Among the Dead Cities
On Religion (*with Mick Gordon)*
Against All Gods
Truth, Meaning and Realism
Towards the Light
The Choice of Hercules

AS EDITOR

Robert Herrick: Lyrics of Love and Desire
Philosophy: A Guide Through the Subject
Philosophy: Further Through the Subject
The Continuum Encyclopaedia of British Philosophy
Schopenhauer's 'Art of Always Being Right'

THE CHOICE OF HERCULES

Pleasure, Duty and the Good Life in the 21st Century

A. C. GRAYLING

PHOENIX

A PHOENIX PAPERBACK

First published in Great Britain in 2007
by Weidenfeld & Nicolson
This paperback edition published in 2008
by Phoenix,
an imprint of Orion Books Ltd,
Orion House, 5 Upper St Martin's Lane,
London WC2H 9EA

An Hachette Livre UK company

1 3 5 7 9 10 8 6 4 2

A CIP catalogue record for this book
is available from the British Library.

ISBN 978-0-7538-2443-6

Printed and bound in the UK by CPI Mackays,
Chatham, Kent

The Orion Publishing Group's policy is to use papers
that are natural, renewable and recyclable products and
made from wood grown in sustainable forests. The logging
and manufacturing processes are expected to conform to
the environmental regulations of the country of origin.

www.orionbooks.co.uk

For Katie

minime hercule!
Ex quo, quantum boni sit in amicitia, iudicari potest

Contents

Preface

As a young man, so the tales have it, the legendary strong-man Hercules was accosted by personifications of Duty and Pleasure in the form of attractive women, each adjuring him to follow her into the life she represented. The story attracted painters, poets and composers of the late Renaissance as emblematic of the crucial juncture all must face in life: nothing less than the fundamental choice of moral orientation and therefore, for Renaissance thinkers and people like them, the ultimate destiny of their immortal souls. One might put it by saying that it represents the dividing of the ways leading respectively to the good life and the Good Life.

Or does it? The connoted dichotomy between the good life – most crudely conceived as one of wine, revel, carelessness, and ease – and the Good Life – the goody two-shoes, moralistic life of duty, self-denial and (often) piety – is a distortion imposed by outlooks most closely associated with the latter. There is a different starting point for thinking about good lives, premised on the realisation that the best of both sides of this spurious dichotomy matter, in alliance with other considerations. That is what this book is about: the idea that certain demands and certain pleasures are necessary, not just because of their intrinsic merits but because of what they do for each other.

This book is therefore a contribution to a history of debate begun by Socrates with his question: how should one live? Many streams of thought have flowed from the challenge in that question, among which the chief three are, first, the later academic tradition, in which close technical analysis of the concepts in play is the chief preoccupation; second, the saccarine and often emetic tradition of uplifting advice and soothing counsel, to be found in books of usually non-standard size and pastel covers; and third, the reflective conversation among those who both know something of the world and think about it, such as Cicero, Montaigne, Shaftesbury, Hume, and the English essayists. With due diffidence this discussion subjoins itself to the last group. What one will not find here is anything drawn from a fourth but tangential tradition, consisting in devotional and exhortatory works of religion.

Two remarks are necessary. First, I would not have anyone think for a moment that the author comes close to living the life described here as good, though – no doubt in common with many who open these pages – he makes intermittent and occasionally strenuous efforts to do so. The consolation for us all is this: that what really matters is the attempt; and when we judge people most generously, what we honour is their aspirations, not only their successes; for if the latter alone counted, how few human beings would merit anything but pity or scorn.

Second, the topic here has many sides, and the Western tradition's efforts to explore and understand it are rich. Between these two facts one has both to select particularities and yet range widely. Accordingly I conceive my task as one of assembling reminders and suggestions, as materials that one can use to build one's own conception of a life truly worth living – both in the judgement and experience of the person living it, and in the judgement and experience of those affected by it. Once only the latter was thought to be a legitimate measure of a life's worth; it brings an ancient but powerful insight back into play to assert the former too.

This is a book for the general reader, and it assumes no prior knowledge in any field of enquiry other than life itself. That precious commodity is instructive stuff, but it is all the better for what Socrates urged: reflection, and consideration, so that the best can be made of it, and found in it.

Introduction

In the quest we undertake for the best possible life we are capable of – an individually tailored best life for each – there has inevitably to be something ideal, and much practical. The ideal is more than the sum of the practical's details, though largely composed of them, for it ought always to have an horizon of striving that lies beyond what we have so far achieved, to serve as the perpetual goal that good lives never lack.

This sounds very earnest, no doubt; as if seeking and living the best life were all effort and striving, all sweat, no fun. Nothing is or should be further from the truth. If enjoyment and fulfilment were not an essential part of a good life, living it would not only be a negative enterprise, but it would be much less use to others, whether intimates or the wider community. If anything, the example of humourless, disapproving, repressive moralisers whose pointing fingers have blighted enough lives to fill armies many times over, ought to be enough to remind us that the phrase 'the good life' genuinely merits its double meaning: for the valuable life (the life truly worth living for the one living it) and the pleasurable life (of which affection, laughter, achievement and beauty are integral characteristics) are one and the same.

It is, or should be, startling to remember that this point, now widely enough accepted in most of what we think of as 'contemporary Western civilisation' to verge on cliché, has not always been the majority view in that civilisation's history, and is not so even now in the world at large. For this view is the diametric opposite of a species of moral outlook for which the value of human life is not located between its beginning in birth and its end in death here in the natural world, but refers to a transcendent realm judged by standards that have relatively little to do with the actualities of worldly existence. Any major religion you care to nominate is premised on this alternative vision, and accordingly it is typical of religion-based moralities to hold that much of what affords pleasure and brings achievement in real human lives is actually a barrier to moral success, and might indeed damn us.

The long-drawn opposition here at issue is the subject of another, although of course related, debate: the debate between religious ethics and what might broadly be called humanistic ethics. I address it in a book called *What Is Good?* Here I start where that debate ends, on the assumption that the case for the humanistic outlook is overwhelming; and therefore the starting point in these pages is the premise that human individuals, as intelligent agents capable of making choices and deciding for themselves what to aim for, are responsible for making the best life possible for themselves in the heres and nows of their time in the world. And their time in the world is brief enough to add urgency to the question, 'How shall we live for the best?' for an average human lifespan is less than a thousand months long.

Given that this responsibility is an individual matter, and personal to each of us, the aim in the following pages is not to legislate or dictate: far from it. Rather, it is to contribute a point of view about some of the general considerations relating to the ideal and the practical aspects of what makes good lives.

Is it really hard to identify and state a general conception of kinds of lives worth living? To repeat: this does not and cannot mean a single prescription that would suit everyone, for there is no such thing; there are as many possible good lives as there are people to choose them, so far as their details and particularities are concerned. But it is indeed possible to offer a general account of what elements enter into the making of good lives, together with some of their defining characteristics in practice. This is an account that draws on considerations about human nature and the human condition – so, a reflective account of each is required – and it responds to questions about the role of luck in the good life, and the fact that all lives are subject to constraints, limitations, obstacles, difficulties, endogenous deficits and exogenous accidents – though the way that some of these are addressed can itself be a component of what makes a life good.

In the first part of the book, therefore, I look at the overall question of what features of lives make them good lives. In the second and third parts, in rather different vein, I describe some moral attitudes to major questions, the kind of attitudes that someone reflecting in this humanistic way might well arrive at on the basis of the connoted general idea of 'the good'. This matters because there cannot be good lives unless they are lived in good societies and (ultimately) in a good world – by which is at least meant societies that are tolerant, intelligent, free, open, peaceful, and just, and a world that is largely likewise.

Between the first and second parts of the book, by way of intermission in both senses of the word, I consider the fact that even the best lives have in them loss and grief, failure and suffering, and I try to say something about how these trials might be faced and overcome. Their overcoming is itself an aspect of living for the best, and is often a source of some of the human heart's finest personal achievements.

For the first part of the book I use as a starting point the Renaissance trope of 'the choice of Hercules' as exemplifying the fundamental moral contrast between two broad types of lives: those lived in pursuit of worldly aims, then too often reductively characterised as 'venal' lives, which is too quickly simplified further into lives aimed at 'pleasure'; and – by contrast, as our ancestors saw it – lives lived 'virtuously', by which was almost exclusively meant obedience to conventional religion-based ideas of moral duty. In the art of the late Renaissance and the Enlightenment, Hercules is depicted as a young man addressed by two women, one of them handsome and the other beautiful (but the beautiful one – in some paintings – has a serpent's tail and clawed feet), respectively representing Virtue or Duty, and Pleasure or Vice. Each tries to persuade Hercules to accompany her to the domain of life she stands for. Hercules of course (consider the epoch) chooses Duty/Virtue, and proceeds to the laborious existence that ends in his being admitted among the immortals on Olympus. Thus he exemplifies official moral doctrine; and thus is the assumption revealed that moral duty and worldly avocations are mutually exclusive, indeed at war with each other, the outcome at stake being nothing less than the fate of the eternal soul.

One should not be misled by what seems a trivialisingly over-neat dichotomy here. Moral arbiters were then confident that they had the high ground in asserting the claims of duty over worldly distractions, and the makers of paintings, poems, and oratorios recounting Hercules' choice of destiny scarcely ever display a need actually to make the case for duty, or to explore the supposedly rival claims of pleasure. The assumptions underlying their use of the myth are interesting, and it is educative to note them.

Yet as the point made above suggests (the near-cliché point about the acceptable ambiguity in the meaning of the phrase 'the good life'), there is no real dichotomy in the choice offered to Hercules. Rather, there is much right on both sides of the putative divide, and much wrong about both. But most importantly, there is much right about the combination of what is right in both. And what is right is the idea of the good life they jointly suggest.

In the second and third parts of the book a change of gear brings into view the surely incontestable thought that good lives cannot be the best they can be unless lived in an appropriate social and political setting. This implies that the kind of good envisaged in good personal lives should also be the basis of attitudes to social questions – including political ones – because what an individual needs in the way of liberty, opportunity, tolerance, and generosity from others in order to realise his or her own best potential, has – in its reciprocal outward projection – definite implications for how we should treat others, and that means how we view important legal, political and social questions.

In the book's second part I restrict attention to some main topics of moral anxiety in contemporary Western society, to show what these implications are. These views were first voiced in a short book entitled *Moral Values*, which in effect I revise, extend, and update here, and which I mention partly by way of a nine o'clock watershed warning, because some of those who read that earlier book thought it would have been better named *Immoral Values*.

All discussions of this kind are no more nor less than contributions to the conversation of mankind. They might hope to be right in every particular, but they ought always to be open to correction if they are not, and to supplementation even if they are. Both correction and supplementation should come from the wider debate of which they are part. In the spirit of these remarks it is appropriate to say that what follows is straightforwardly meant and modestly proposed, and stands ready to be corrected or supplemented whenever reason and truth dictate.

PART I
The Individual Good

CHAPTER 1

The Myth of the Choice of Hercules

A curiosity attaches to the use of the myth of Hercules' youthful choice between Duty and Pleasure, or Virtue and Vice – the terms were taken to be interchangeable, though in the myth's most famous first telling it was the second pair that figured. The curiosity is that Hercules was scarcely an example of the choice he is said to have made, namely, Duty or Virtue. His legends together represent him as a brawling hooligan, a multiple murderer, an anarchy of brawn and appetite conjoined – far from the thoughtful individual, chin in hand, listening attentively to the arguments and blandishments of the two charming advocates who present their cases to him.

Indeed, the reason that Hercules is working as a cowherd in a rural fastness at the time Duty and Pleasure find him is that he has murdered his music tutor, the hapless Linus, and his earthly stepfather has banished him to pastoral duties as a penitence. While herding cows Hercules was entertained by Thespius, father of fifty daughters, all of whom Hercules proceeded to sleep with – in some versions, all of them in a single night; in others, one per night. In this latter version the girls were supplied to Hercules' couch by Thespius himself, because the old man could recognise sterling genes when he saw them. Hercules was, after all, the natural son of Zeus himself, the outcome of one of the god's many dalliances with mortal women, in this case Alcmene. (The Christian story is another retelling of this ancient myth about gods, mortal maids, and resulting heroes. It is a trope that far pre-dates Zeus.)

The classic version of the tale of Hercules' choice appears in the *Memorabilia* of Xenophon. Xenophon was a friend and pupil of Socrates as well as a distinguished writer and military man in his own right. In his *Memorabilia* he has Socrates recount the anecdote as if it had been told him by someone else – as it happens, by Prodicus, Socrates' teacher. It goes as follows. As Hercules sat watching his herd, a tall, slender woman in a simple white robe approached him from one side, while from the other came a curvaceous young woman in make-up and plunging décolletage. The latter offered Hercules sex, entertainment, and lifelong ease; the former offered him struggle and labour, rewarded by immortal fame. Socrates does not explicitly say which way Hercules decided, but of course we gather that he chose undying fame and all that led to it as the only right and possible course for a deity's son with a high destiny.

The story is too good ever to have been neglected in subsequent moral and even political symbolisations. It was applied to different heroes; Scipio had a dream very like it, which inspired Rome, and it was incorporated into Christian teaching (one reworking of it has Christ in the wilderness for forty days, but with only one would-be seducer). Poussin, Veronese, Paolo de Matteis and Rubens painted it; Handel and Bach put it to music; the revolutionary fathers of the United States wanted to represent it on their coinage; and the French revolutionaries proposed to build a giant statue of virtue-choosing Hercules in central Paris as an emblem of their new order.

One aspect of the power of the story is that with his muscles and half-divine birth, Hercules could have lived mightily whichever of the options he chose; so by opting for duty and virtue, by seeking deathless fame rather than decadent gratification and ease, this prodigious figure bent his strength to the direction of good – a super role model (a role supermodel?) especially for restless, randy, aggressive, testosterone-soaked young adult males in all the phases of history in which the myth was used as a morality tale.

It is entertaining to see how the Enlightenment handled the story. The libretto for Handel's oratorio *The Choice of Hercules* (HWV 69, 1761) was drawn from a poem by Robert Lowth and adapted by Handel's librettist Thomas Morell. The adaptation weakened the moral punch of Lowth's original by its abridgements and its substitutions of terms, principally 'pleasure' in place of Lowth's 'sloth'. But in fact it thereby reached back, no doubt inadvertently, to something closer to the original intention of the tale; for in the Greek outlook there would have been little point in pitting an obviously winning argument against one of equally obvious demerit, and in any case pleasure was not regarded by the Greeks with the squeamish horror of Christian moralisers, for whom it was one of the enemies who fling wide the gates to Satan.

In Handel's oratorio Pleasure offers Hercules a home on 'yonder myrtle plain', where streams glide, the smoking feast is being prepared, and her 'laughing train' wait to serve him. Perfumes suffuse the cool, shady bower, and its peace is enhanced by 'sweet warbling lays' to love and beauty. And nearby waits Beauty herself, aglow for his arms:

> Love awakes its purest fire
> And to each ravish'd sense bestows
> All that can raise or sate desire.

Enthused, the chorus cries, 'Seize, seize these blessings, blooming boy.'

Virtue will have none of it. 'Away mistaken wretch, away!' she sternly says to Pleasure,

> spread your snare elsewhere ...
> This manly youth's exalted mind
> Above thy grovelling taste refin'd
> Shall listen to my awful voice.

To Hercules she promises 'the golden trump of fame' when he has bared his breast and poured out his 'generous blood' for his country.

Virtue does not have it quite all her own way in Handel. Hercules addresses Pleasure as 'enchanting Siren', and is half seduced by her delicious blandishments, all the more enticing for promising Love as the reward for choosing her. At one point he says, 'Oh, whither reason dost thou fly?/Purge the soft charm that fascinates my eye.' He is struggling. Virtue's response is to exhort him to 'Mount, mount the steep ascent' – here is an allusion to the familiar Christian conceit of the strait and narrow way – 'and claim thy native skies!' Hercules at last obeys her, choosing to be 'a god among the gods' in return for forfeiting the life of pleasure for a life of trial, forgoing amorousness for arduousness, ease for labour, the present for the future.

Librettist and composer between them give Pleasure some of the best lines and airs; Virtue's victory is an unpersuasive one in Handel's rendering, but of course convention unloads its great weight into her side of the scales, and Handel's contemporaries would have known what they were supposed to believe, even if they did not really believe it, or want to.

But it matters that something better than winding streams and sexual promise should be made out for pleasure's argument, because in all but the starved conception of the good life that various pieties seek to impose, pleasure is one of its essentials – pleasure, that is to say, well understood. So we must ask: what is pleasure, when well understood?

What pleases, what affords delight, what satisfies the human need for taste, colour, sensation, stimulation, distraction, thereby adding relish to our hours and making our days happy, is obviously enough a peculiarly mixed bag. The large differences in personal tastes explain why, but so also does the fact that although many people can learn to be satisfied with a narrow and unvarying repertoire of interests, equally many cannot, at least for long; that is a function of the sheer fact of human intelligence.

It follows not merely that there is no single formula for encapsulating what life's pleasures are, but – more importantly – that there should not be, though philosophers have plunged themselves into trouble by trying to legislate about both. Epicurus, founder of the Epicurean school in the third century BC, taught that the true pleasures are those of intellectual discourse and friendship; that the highest enjoyment is attained by sitting in the shade discussing philosophy, and otherwise living with simplicity and moderation. 'Epicurean' has come to denote something quite different, indeed opposite: a life of luxury, drink, feasting – in short, sensual indulgence; and it is this that Handel's Pleasure invokes. This happened because Epicurus' outlook was summed up in the adjuration to 'pursue pleasure and avoid pain', and coarser sensibilities fail to recognise that what they think pleasurable is precisely what Epicurus regarded as containing the seeds of pain, given that the fruits of sensual excess are indigestion, hangover, obesity, illness, and so dismally on. Epicurus' other slogan, 'moderation in all things', guarded against this. It did, however, include moderation itself; so the Epicureans occasionally let their hair down and had a party.

'True pleasure': the implication of the adjective for John Stuart Mill, more than two thousand years after Epicurus, was much the same. He distinguished between higher and lower pleasures, thereby attracting much criticism from those who do not see how anything but a certain kind of prejudice, however well meaning, can assert the superiority of reading Aeschylus to having a pint of beer in a pub. Mill responded by saying that someone who knew both pleasures was in the right position to judge which was the 'higher'; but this does not silence his critics, who in sum say that either there is an implicit intellectual snobbery in the view, or that someone who knew both pleasures could nevertheless still prefer beer to Aeschylus – and on what grounds could one reproach him?

It is inevitable that someone who claims to be in a position to recognise the respect in which a Jane Austen novel is superior to a Mills and Boon novel (they both have roughly the same basic plot: boy meets girl, vicissitudes ensue, vicissitudes are resolved, boy marries girl), or the respect in which a Beethoven symphony is superior to a pop song, is going to invite just such a challenge, and rightly so; for one thing, the point is not only about the intrinsic merits of what is being compared in each case, but also about the value to those who encounter them. For some, a pint of beer is more valuable, more interesting, more attractive than a reading of Aeschylus. For some, a Mills and Boon novel is more accessible, more assimilable, and more enjoyable than the intricacies and ironies of Jane Austen and her delicate prose. A Beethoven symphony might be an agony to someone for whom the driving rhythms of a pop song, and its lyrics addressing matters of immediate interest to his or her youthful romances, are manna. Granting all this is to take a wider view of what pleasure legitimately and necessarily embraces.

For my money the complexity, depth, nuance, power, and insight of Jane Austen, Beethoven and Aeschylus knock the putative competitors into a cocked hat. But that's for my money; and this is not the point in discussing the role of pleasure in making life good. It would be a hideous distortion of the endeavour to encourage good lives if things that give pleasure were to be denied people on supposed elitist grounds, or in the belief that Mill is right – though he is – about 'higher pleasures'. So what? The point is not about the altitude of pleasure, but its existence; and that refocuses the question from the supposed nature of the pleasure to what it does. As adding to the good of an individual existence, this is as it should be. If pleasure is actually an Epicurean seed of pain, that raises a question about it that must be discussed, for if we think, as we well might, that this makes a future-pain-promising current pleasure intrinsically un-desirable (smoking, binge drinking, unprotected sex), it abuts the question of the individual's freedom, another of the essentials of the good life (see later). If it harms others, it is definitely illegitimate – for the harm principle, which states that it is never right to do what harms others, except in clearly justified circumstances such as self-defence and the prevention of greater harm, trumps everything. All these points are surely obvious enough.

Pleasure has a twofold possibility: there is mental pleasure, and there is pleasure both mental and physical. Consider the second first. Pleasure as conscious enjoyment of the human sensory endowment – the reflective ability to contemplate, anticipate, remember, and heighten the experience of the senses, in appreciation of music, the taste and effects of food and drink, enjoyment of sex, the pleasure of dancing, swimming, lying in the sun, walking in the country, having a massage, and so variously and multiply on – would doubtless be pleasurable enough in the moment as a purely physical thing ('animal pleasure' we sometimes say), but it is obvious that reflexive consciousness of the fact that pleasurable stimulation of some combination of senses is occurring adds greatly to their effect. Think of the opposite: the way that pain or discomfort is heightened by anticipation and tension. The key to understanding pleasure as a central good is to see how it fits with a conception of humanity contrasted to views describing the senses and their pleasures as traps and snares, portals through which evil comes.

One of the foremost results of renewed interest in art, literature and philosophy in the brilliant epoch we call the Renaissance was its fostering of an intelligent interest in human existence in the ordinary world, not for any instrumental purpose of salvation or a posthumous destiny in another world, but for life in the here and now, in this world, for its own sake. The chief mark of this was the appearance of a number of dissertations and essays on the subject of 'the dignity of man', starting with that great obstetrician of the Renaissance, Petrarch, and including Gianozzo Manetti's *On the Excellency and Dignity of Man* (a direct reply to Pope Innocent III's *On the Misery of Man*) and Pico Della Mirandola's *Oration on the Dignity of Man*. Their principal aim was to challenge the prevailing view of medieval theology that human existence in this world is a dangerous, temporary travail, a time of test and suffering, in which the devil and his agents are constantly working to snatch away immortal souls. By rigorous adherence to his duty and denial of the flesh, which is Satan's entrance, a man could escape and achieve heaven at last. In the gloomy and intentionally minatory Christian *contemptus mundi* literature of the medieval period, each stage of life was represented as a site of tribulation, from the vulnerability of childhood to the infirmity and decay of age. The agonies of the flesh, hunger and desire, disease, accident and injury, fear and worry, poverty and tyranny, were all depicted with macabre relish by the propagandists of this desperate outlook, to scare people into obedience to the Church and the temporal powers, an unholy and mutually convenient combination.

The response of humanism was to celebrate man's reason, and the possibility of beauty in the body. Man's reason equated him to the gods, and gave him power over things in the world. Animals are enslaved by their nature, condemned to eat one kind of food just in those parts of nature that supply it, and to follow blindly the cycle of their instincts. A human being can choose where to live, and can take his sustenance and provision from the variety of nature. He might not have the teeth of the tiger, the strength of the elephant, the pelt of the bear, but he can make spears as sharp as the tiger's tooth, can organise himself into hunting parties stronger in their combination than the elephant, can clothe himself in the furs and skins of the creatures he hunts. And add to this his power of speech, with its infinite capacity to bring past and future into the present, and to span the world and the heavens with the wings it gives to his powers of imagination.

Perhaps the most marked departure from the Christian writers of the period labelled by Petrarch 'the middle ages' (because, he said, they threw a shadow over the interval between the brilliance of the classical past and the new age which drew its reviving inspiration from it) was the Renaissance's lively appreciation of the body itself. For Christian moralists, the body was a betrayer, constantly threatening to revolt against the soul's best interests, with its appetites and urgencies, its temptations and scarcely containable desires. Ascetes whipped and scourged themselves, wore hair shirts and thorns, starved, even cut off their genitals. Origen, who famously 'made himself a eunuch for the Kingdom of Heaven', came to regret doing so; but he was far from alone among those who took drastic measures to subdue the flesh.

Humanists rejected these perversions. Instead they celebrated physical beauty, in paintings and poems, in their ethics and lives. They deeply appreciated the point of classical proportionings, in the spirit of Protagoras' view that 'man is the measure of all things', which implied that houses, public buildings, townscapes, the very organisation of daily life, should reflect the human scale. They especially approved of the writings of Lactantius and Cicero that urged these principles, and (as it happened incorrectly) praised the fact that human beings were the only creatures with an upright posture, enabling them to look at the heavens, which they saw as a mark of his exalted nature and excellence.

Petrarch and his successors in the humanist tradition were not, of course, secularists in the sense that the later use of 'humanism' has come to entail, so they expressed themselves in a modified and refocused religious language, concentrating on such things as God's assumption of human form to transact his New Testament with mankind, and on the teaching that God had made man in his own image – hence man's beauty and fineness – and had even given man a godlike mandate over the world of nature. But above all, the fact that man was a concretion of body and soul meant that he was the very lynchpin of creation, joining and bridging the world of matter, time and mortality to the eternal world of truth and the spirit. This was in fact a revival of Neoplatonist doctrine dating from a millennium earlier, but it exactly suited humanist preoccupations. One of the most enthusiastic revivers of this outlook was Marsilio Ficino. As well as viewing humanity as the link point between earth and heaven, Ficino saw man as emblematic of creation, as, indeed, the microcosm, which is to say: the universe in little. This idea came from Plato's *Timaeus*, one of the few works of Plato known to all generations since it was written, so its doctrines had been much cited, but in the Renaissance it took on a revived and added significance. Much metaphysics went into making out what it implied; one suggestion was that man must be regarded as the microcosm because he consists of the same elements – earth, air, fire and water – as the macrocosm. Paracelsus taught that man was the knot tying earth and heaven because he conjoined to these four a fifth element, which was divine: the 'quintessence'.

In his *Oration on the Dignity of Man*, Pico Della Mirandola introduced an important shift into the developing picture of what it is to be human. He said that human beings have the capacity to make of themselves whatever they desired. This took humanity out of the lynchpin position at the centre of the Great Chain of Being, conceived as stretching from the lowliest existing things on one side – worms and insects – to the deity himself on the other side. Instead it emphasised man's freedom, an agent in creation rather than a placeholder in its structure. Pico backed this claim by citing God's licence to Adam to act as he saw fit with regard to what he had been given – namely, dominion over the sublunary world.

Pico's view was influential in his own time, and has remained so ever since; indeed, it has grown in significance, recapturing the concept of individual autonomy – central to ethics – and even existential solitude, an idea that plays a central role in most forms and periods of a broadly romantic inspiration. In an extended application of the former concept it has influenced all thinking about individuality, involving in particular a growing appreciation of the place of the individual in society, and the relations of power, wealth and rights that determine it. When it was believed that heaven has the first call on everything of value to human existence, it was of relatively little importance to answer questions about what human beings are and what they need in order to flourish in the here and now. As soon as attention is turned to this latter matter, a large number of deeply significant considerations come suddenly into view, about rights, justice, education, the proper organisation of society to serve the ends of human flourishing, and more – in the ideal, all bent towards making the good human life possible in the natural course of a human lifetime, in this world, now.

Given this, it is not too much to say that Pico's reconfiguring of our view of humanity is one of the most crucial nodes in the more recent history of ethics, reviving as it does the Greek conception that because the interest of the individual in the embodied life is central, things of this life such as pleasure and beauty are, along with the government of reason, essentials of lives worth living.

CHAPTER 2

The Notes of the Good

And so we turn to the question itself: what is the good life? In one sense the answer is obvious enough. It is the well-lived life, the meaningful life, the fulfilled life. Saying this is, however, scarcely likely to be controversial because it is, though at the very least true, obviously too general. Ethical enquiry should issue in substantive suggestions for what meaning and fulfilment are; even better, it should provide practical suggestions for applying those substantive suggestions to the practice of actual life, lived in the way actual lives are lived: among ordinariness, demands, complexities, obstacles, accidents, setbacks, opportunities, good luck and bad, other people, limitations, weariness, tribulations, joys, and an existing framework of institutions and social practices which themselves constrain part (and often much) of the possibilities that most individuals can reasonably expect to actualise.

In light of this the attempt to say something useful about the nature of the good life seems a big challenge indeed, if not positively hubristic. But there are in fact many helps to hand for doing so, to be drawn from the rich and magnificent traditions of thought on this subject in the great civilisations, not least Western civilisation. Few these days would consistently subscribe to any single one of the ethical schools that have existed in those traditions, for the good reason that in the world bequeathed by the Enlightenment we do not think the point is to submit to the dictates of a system, but instead to learn from the best systems for our own individual purposes. Or at least, this is what inheritors of Enlightenment attitudes think, for Enlightenment – as Immanuel Kant famously taught – is a process, not a state, namely the process of thinking for oneself, and therefore living autonomously.

Of course there are still many today, too many, who submit to systems, which means letting the systems do their choosing and thinking for them; and given that almost all these systems were devised in the remote past, they can be made to fit modern conditions only by much bending, temporising, reinterpretation, and straightforward hypocrisy. To people trapped in, or who are voluntary followers of, such systems, the invitation stands to free themselves and join those who think for themselves. If they wish to remain among their convictions they must of course be free to do so, providing they do no harm to others (a provision which convictions of that kind rarely, alas, observe).

The intention here is not to rehearse the teachings of the great traditions, but to distil and apply their lessons, by working onwards from some of the values they identified, the goals and goods they extolled, and the style of living they enjoined – in each selecting the best that speak to us and answer to our condition. One might consider setting up these best choices as ideals to aspire to, in arrangements and among practicalities we can manage. This suggestion would pass muster, if postulating ideals and indicating the straight way towards them did not carry a suggestion of inevitable incompletion and even failure. For to speak of ideals in the context of practical life, though not without merit, is also not without drawbacks. Ordinary practical life is scarcely ever ideal, or a place where ideals are realised. Ordinary practical life is an alloy, mixed with much dross, and the task is to make it good by making it the best it can be in its circumstances, with the endeavour itself being part of that good. To suggest that life is good if (only if?) it is ideal or perfect, rather than to suggest that one achieves the good by living a process – the process of working towards one's ideals – is to misuse the concept of the ideal. And since we mostly do thus misuse it, an alternative way of expressing the point would be better.

In place of talking about ideals, therefore, one might instead talk of the *notes* that could be sounded in a life of aspiration to the good. I intend an analogy to musical notes, to resonances, to the key in which a life is set. What is sought is a certain effect or quality, as when as assemblage of notes sounded on an instrument produces a harmony. When Aristotle spoke of *eudaimonia* – well-doing and well-being, flourishing, a sense of fittingness and achievement in the course of daily life – he had something analogous in mind. In his ethics the life whose path is chosen by reason, the highest human faculty, is a life with this overall characteristic quality, which attends living as light attends fire, or as a musical key generates a distinctive harmonic atmosphere – bright like C major, or muted like C minor.

There are at least seven notes that aspiration to the best life might seek to sound: the note of *meaning*, the note of *intimacy*, the note of *endeavour*, the note of *truth*, the note of *freedom*, the note of *beauty*, and the note of *fulfilment*. This list doubtless looks (as well as pretentious) rather ambitious – and to be frank, so it is. But given that it is at the same time a list of things actually realisable in daily human existence, it does (or should) also sound inviting.

By the first note, the note of meaning, is meant the identification of values and goals. By the second, the note of intimacy, is meant our deepest personal connections, as essentially social beings, in relationship with others. By the third, the note of endeavour, is meant the activity of building and furnishing what is required for the life one has chosen, according to one's values. By the fourth, the note of truth, is meant the determination to live with intellectual honesty, respecting evidence and the canons of rationality. By the fifth, the note of freedom, is meant autonomy, self-government and taking responsibility for one's choices, so that one's life is one's own. By the sixth, the note of beauty, is meant the circumambient quality of the setting of one's life. And by the last, the note of fulfilment, is meant the achievement of integrating the other six into a whole which one recognises as constituting one's own chosen project for the good.

The same problem affects describing these notes as hinders attempts to give a straightforward definition of the good life itself: one would end in generalisations, and (worse) they might sound prescriptive rather than descriptive. So the method I employ is to speak about some of what the notes respectively sound like, so that each might add what would complete a chord for himself – or to vary the metaphor: the method might be likened to scattering pieces of a jigsaw from which each might begin to construct his own picture, a different picture for each. To adopt this method is not evasion; it is forced by the complexity of the details, and by the autonomy of individuals.

The note of meaning concerns the identification of values and the goals they specify. One thought prompted by the word 'goals' is that it contains the idea of process, or a journey. One is situated here, and the goal lies over there; a route must be plotted between them, and choices made about what equipment is required for the journey. The latter might typically be education, but in any case some appropriate form of preparation and supply.

A variant is to think of oneself as the author of a narrative, specifically, one's autobiography. There are those who are emphatic in rejecting such an idea, saying that because stories have beginnings, middles and ends, one would thus be living like a dead person, because termination is essential to a tale, and settles its shape. They thereby intend to urge the claims of chance and accident in individuality. They are of course right about this latter, but mistaken about living narratively; for to have goals and to pursue them is not to be blind to unexpected eventualities and the dramatic alterations of direction they prompt. To have no goals is to be adrift, waiting for other people's choices and journeys to barge one aside, or drag one along, or submerge one in their wake. To have goals and to be working towards them at every point of one's life, even if they change, is always to have direction and purpose, always to be moving under one's own steam.

The meat of the matter, of course, lies in the question of what goals to choose. Whatever they are, they will be chosen because they are or embody the values, desires, hopes and forms of self-definition which, by selecting and living in accordance with them, constitute life's meaning. This is the interesting part. Think of identifying these goals by asking a question that would bring them to light. There is a suggestion – indeed, a dramatisation – made more than once in the philosophical tradition about how one would recognise the values that most speak to one. This is by challenging people to ask themselves the question, 'Should I or should I not commit suicide?' If one answers No, as the great majority of us would, it is because there are things worth doing, being and having – values worth living for. And then the question 'What are they?' becomes easier to answer.

As this indirectly implies, different individuals will choose a different set of things that make them answer No to the suicide question, though it will be no surprise if the sets considerably overlap. There is another dramatic way of speaking about what ought to belong in any such set. Because the universe exists as the outcome of morally neutral physical forces, without being the expression of a purpose and without imposing on individual consciousnesses any external demand or aim, people themselves have to impose on to this radical neutrality their own best conception of values. And these, so some have plausibly suggested, are the freedom and dignity of the individual, friendship and love, and creativity. Aspiring to realise these things in one's life is a powerful value-creating endeavour.

In fact, one can say something stronger about these chosen values: that they are indeed essentials. Without freedom it is impossible to make choices that are one's own, and therefore a life that is one's own construction. Autonomy – self-governance – is the kernel of freedom, and as such reveals what is implied: that the mind is freedom's first theatre. No one can imprison it if it does not choose to be imprisoned, though of course most minds live in the narrowest of prisons – of convention, religion, ignorance, laziness. As one acutely perceptive observer of the human condition put it, 'Most people are other people' – that is, most people live borrowed lives because they borrow their opinions, their emotions, their goals and beliefs, from others, for they either do not know how to make and have their own, or are too timid to venture making and having their own. To dare to think for oneself, carefully; and to stand by one's conclusions, bravely; and to change one's mind in the face of better arguments or convincing evidence, honestly: these are the marks of freedom, the emblems of autonomy, and they are a constitutive part of meaning because they are its responsible and serious underpinning, which casts value on to the things chosen in that very endeavour.

It is easy to write 'friendship' and 'love' in any shortlist of components of meaning, partly because their obviousness makes one think that the words alone are enough. It is scarcely bearable to think what a life without either would be like – and such lives are lived by some, who learn to cara-pace themselves, growing a cyst around the loneliness that eventually, in the majority of those cases, shows what direc-tions the stunted heart takes: eccentric, self-addressing, in-ward. It has been said that people wrapped up in themselves make very small parcels, that empty hearts have room for nothing while full hearts always have room for more – these truths of course bear on the point directly. But think of the positive: how a pair of friends add up to more than two, how expansive and generous the other-directed affections are in their normal functioning; how much there is to learn, and how much pleasure exists, in the symbiosis of people who like and enjoy each other.

There is much demand for creativity both in freedom and in friendship, but the point of singling it out is that the satisfaction of adding something to the world's stock is a profound one, and of them all, creativity is the most immediately and obviously meaningful in itself. We are apt to think that writing a novel, painting a picture, and throw-ing a pot (in the sense of shaping clay on a wheel, not the domestic-quarrel version) are paradigms of creativity, and so they are, but so too are things like bringing up children, starting a business, organising a fête, painting the flats for an amateur theatrical event, singing in a choir, learning to play the piano – in short, exercising the ingenuity and talent that is the genetic endowment of all human beings, those intelligent and diverse primates for whom such avocations are the reason for being – quite literally so, given that they are expressions of the supreme human adaptation.

I speak of all these things again in the following pages, and in more detail. At this point it is relevant to say that the richest philosophical resource for exploring ideas about meaning is literature – the novel, the drama, poetry. Literature is many other things besides, of course, but one typical aspect of it is that it explores such questions as what one should do, and how one should choose, in the situations of dilemma and conflict they construct. The philosophical endeavour is especially marked when a premise is the absence of externally imposed meaning in the world, which implies a need to strive to project value on to life, a striving itself constitutive of the good – for as the cliché has it (no less truly for being one), the journey matters as much as the destination.

One could do worse than be persuaded by this or similar views, but the point of citing them is not to urge their acceptance so much as to indicate a line of thought. And attending that line of thought is another, roughly of the form: 'Go and try it.'

Everyone has a set of values, most of them rather hazily defined and incompletely observed, inherited from their upbringings, from the legacies of religious instruction, and from the Babel of voices in the media and society over whatever happens to be the latest moral panic. The first task is to take these derived values out of their half-closed drawers, dust them off, and subject them to rigorous and unsparingly honest appraisal. It would again be unsurprising if quite a few of them went straight into the wastepaper basket. Given the nature of conventional and religious moralities, the basket might indeed fill rapidly if the scrutiny were truly thorough. And then one could begin afresh, demanding a case to be made for each putative value, in the full light of reason.

The promise is that out of this will come a sense of what is important for oneself that serves as a compass-setting to navigate by, in the form of recognising things really worth doing, being or having. Once that conviction is in place, it gives shape to one's life; once the pursuit has been embarked upon, it floods life with value.

The other notes in the list are not separate from the note of meaning, but constitutive of it. There is no significance in the order in which some considerations about each are now mentioned, although it feels natural to turn again and immediately to the note of intimacy – or more generally: relationship, though it is close relationships that matter most in making lives meaningful; so this is more than the general point about friendship and affection, but about the best and deepest kinds of both.

And here one makes a statement of the obvious, given that human beings are essentially – of the essence – social animals. A large part of each individual's character and outlook is shaped by the nature of the relationships he or she has, for good and ill; a point worth stressing, though familiar, because relationships can warp, poison, cause misery, and stand as a barrier to the growth of gifts and the taking of opportunities, as well as being sources of good. On the evidence it would seem that it is all too common for people to be harmed and limited by their relationships, not least because conventional and mainly religious moralities dictate their form, and because the exigencies take the infinitely possible child and turn it into the narrowly con-strained adult – constrained as to choices and capacities, after much squeezing of the too familiar kinds embodied in mediocre education and coercive social expectation.

But in the absence of relationships altogether, when solitary and self-enclosed, individuals add up to far less than one. This is not to say that it is better to remain in toxic relationships than to be alone; solitude can for a time be a strengthening and cleansing thing. Rather, it is to say that it is better (again obviously) to be in good relationships than in none. Good relationships are, first, chosen ones; and second, ones that add to each party to them – in terms of their outlook, their emotional strength, their knowledge, their capacities, their enjoyment, their sense of well-being and security, and their interest in doing well in their endeavours.

The point about good relationships being chosen relationships is central. The primary case of such relationships occurs when we encounter people we wish to see more of because of their interest and merits, and the positive chemistry we feel in being with them. So we arrange matters accordingly, and invest effort in tending the developing acquaintanceship. In the case of romantic attachments much more biology underlies the chemistry, but the desired terminus – the rooting of affection, mutuality, on a long-term basis – has the same formal properties.

Most though not all of the more intimate relationships are voluntary ones such as these. But people also find themselves of necessity in many involuntary relationships, in families and in workplaces, and in society at large. In some ways these latter are more testing. Both have an underpinning of obligation, which only enters genuinely chosen relationships when they have matured enough. The large difference between obligatory family relationships and obligatory work ones is that the former have the additional powerful helps of biology at a different point: the tie of kinship, the naturally prompted affections of parent for child, and the dependence of child on parent. Sibling relationships might be full of tension, irritation and rivalry in many circumstances, but because they share so much, not least of memory and early experience, and certainly their unique triangulation upon their parents, they can eventually become rich relationships too, especially in adult life.

The target of success in all relationships is the one extolled with such eloquence by Aristotle in the *Nichomachean Ethics*, namely, friendship.

Aristotle distinguishes genuine friendship from two imitations of it, in one of which the motive for the relationship is pleasure, and in the other of which it is mutual utility. These are superficial relationships which last only as long as their usefulness for the purposes they serve, Aristotle said, in contrast to real friendship, which lasts because it is 'grounded in good'. By this Aristotle meant that the premise of the tie is that each wishes for the other what is genuinely best for him or her. Aristotle described this kind of friendship as 'perfected' or 'completed' because its purpose, its reason for existing, is located wholly within the relationship itself; the relationship is not merely a means to some further good beyond itself.

For Aristotle a friend is 'another self', in the straightforward sense that the concern and interest one feels for one's own well-being is exactly the concern and interest one feels for the friend's well-being. Concern for one's own interests is of course entirely appropriate – one has a duty to look after one's own interests, and moreover (said Aristotle) it encourages one to act nobly, and to make thoughtful decisions about one's choices and commitments. Regarding a friend as another self extends this domain of special concern to include him or her; to treat friends as other selves is accordingly always to will the best for them, for one literally shares their interests.

Aristotle's ideal of friendship is highly personal and mutual, and because he conceived it in these terms it follows that it is also exclusive. Not all philosophers agreed: Immanuel

Kant held that the virtuous individual will extend friendship to all others equally, and can quite legitimately expect reciprocity of pleasure and utility. Søren Kierkegaard had a Christian ground for rejecting Aristotle's view, namely, that because one has been commanded to love all one's neighbours, friendships that exclude any, or distinguish between them, are impermissible.

Actually these opinions are not inconsistent with what Aristotle says. There is no reason why one cannot entertain benevolent feelings towards the rest of humankind, and make efforts for its good, nor that one cannot legitimately expect reciprocal pleasure and usefulness from most of one's acquaintances, and at the same time have deep friendships, in Aristotle's particular sense, with a chosen few. The key thing for him is that friendship of this latter kind has, as its very point and essence, the relationship itself. How could people be good friends to their lovers, families, and most intimate comrades, unless they gave these closest friends more of themselves than they give to strangers, even granting responsibility to these latter too? Friendship at its most genuine is by nature particular, because its focus lies in individual things, in confidences, in understood mutualities. Having too many such would, Aristotle thought, make each one worth less.

However desirable it is to have neat definitions of important ideas – and Aristotle had caught from Socrates the itch to have as neat a set of definitions of the great ideas as possible – the fact is that most of them are too internally complex to be caught in a formula, and 'friendship' is one such. There are many kinds of friendship, achieved by many different routes, and the most they have in common is that – somewhere in the ideal version of them – loyalty, sympathy and affection standardly figure.

Despite Aristotle, not everyone agrees that friendship

is the summit of human relationship. Literature and the movies conspire to give this place to romantic love, while another convention yields the distinction to parent–child relationships. But each of these is successful only if it matures into friendship at last, which is why sages of quite different traditions extol friendship as the highest, the most central, the most necessary link in the social web. Given that humans are – to repeat, as one always must – essentially social beings, having friends thus turns out to be a defining component of life worth living.

It is an interesting coincidence, and perhaps more, that Mencius in ancient China resembled Aristotle in teaching that a friend is 'another self'. If one cares fully about another person, he likewise argued, his good matters as much to oneself as one's own; so a pair of true friends are 'one mind in two bodies'.

Most will justifiably think that this overstates the case, except in those rare iconic instances glorified in literature – David and Jonathan, Nisus and Euryalus – which are nevertheless examples (in the latter case expressly so) of love more romantic than companionate. But it reflects the way that friendship embodies not just camaraderie and enjoyment, but a mutual bond, which at its best, and during its best period, is supportive, forgiving, and durable. Among other things this means that a friend is one who knows when to help you by telling the truth, and when to help you by lying. As Oscar Wilde put it, 'A friend is one who stabs you in the front.'

Nothing can count as friendship which lacks time and a few real tests behind it. Too many acquaintanceships are dignified by the name without having earned it. But friendships do not fail to count as such because they end; sometimes people who were friends in the fullest and richest sense cease to be so after a time, for any number of reasons, usually bad ones.

Friendship is the ultimate aim of parenting too, for the mark of success here must ultimately be to produce independent adults capable of managing themselves in life. A mark of success in this would be the development of genuine friendship between parent and grown-up offspring. If either party tries to prolong aspects of the parent–young-child relationship beyond the end of adolescence, the result is typically unfortunate; the oppressive, meddling, over-interventive parent, or the still-dependent adult offspring, make for toxic partners – unless there is a happy coincidence of needs between the two sides in these respects. But if so, that can scarcely be healthy. People need to form new dependencies, chosen ones, with new partners and spouses different from the dependencies of childhood. There is something crucial in the idea of one kind of separation between parents and offspring in this respect, even if in other respects – the help that parents typically wish to give with grandchildren, and with some of the financial burdens of early adulthood – certain voluntary prolongations of obligation are given scope.

Ties establish themselves between people who work together, although they did not choose each other as individuals at the outset. Comradeship is the name typically given to such ties, denoting a certain loyalty and collegial spirit. However characterised, there is much more between colleagues than between chance strangers on the street, even if there is no liking as such, and no contact outside work. Work is a fruitful place for conflict and dislike, emphasising again, if doing so were needed, the value of chosen relationships. But endeavouring to be a constructive colleague, or at least to manage and minimise friction, is a not insignificant moral challenge, among other things in being educative about our limitations.

Good relationships make us better people: that is the obvious yet important truth in all this. The point comes fully into its own when one endeavours to answer the question: what does one do, speaking generally, when things go wrong with the grand project of working to construct a good life? Those failures of intention, those breakdowns in relationships, those mistakes and bad tempers and arguments, those infidelities and untruths, those feelings of anger and dislike, those defeats and losses, all represent derailments of the project for which one is responsible; they are one's own fault or part-fault. It is not the same with life's vicissitudes – the bad things that happen from beyond one's choices, and outside one's control; for them fortitude, and the task of finding a changed route back to one's better intentions, are what is called for. But to know oneself to be to blame, even in part, for the derailment: that offers a different challenge.

Or does it? In one good sense, fortitude and finding a way either to get back to the chosen path or to forge a new path that also heads in the right direction, represent the same task as when trouble enters from without. But it might also be that there is something personal to the failure in question – the incompleteness of one's efforts to be the person one would like to be might issue in, say, a family quarrel and a breach, full of anger and resentment, and fault. Such things are, alas, commonplace.

So too is the hard-nosed advice relevant to such situations. The first thing to remember is the Greek attitude to moral failure: that it is a case of having made a bad shot, as when you aim at a target and miss. In some moral dispensations the view taken of moral failure is that it leaves a permanent blemish, and has to be worked off, expiated, or forgiven – in a characteristic case (that of Christianity) at the discretion of another agency; there is nothing one can oneself do to wash away the stain. But the Greek attitude was as simple as it was straightforward: if you make a bad shot, you try again, and try better.

For example: suppose one has fallen out with someone, and the breach is unhealable. One might well repine and regret, but obviously that cannot be how things remain. The answer might best be to accept that the relationship is over, and to try better, in other relationships, not to allow what can cause breaches to grow. The lesson is: take better aim next time. Of course one might wish, and try, to heal the breach, and sometimes repaired relationships ('re-paired' seems to be the *mot juste*) can be stronger than they were before they failed. But if they cannot be healed, they can nevertheless teach their lessons for other and different relationships. Not all relationships succeed, and one can still be a good friend, a good lover, a good parent, a good neighbour, despite having failed in any of those categories with other people at other times. The proof is in second marriages that work; if it were true that a failed relationship implied a permanent disability to have a successful relationship, there could be no happy second marriages. Yet they exist.

Another thing worth remembering is that culpable failure in one of the respects at issue – culpable in the sense that one is oneself at fault or partly at fault – often enough means that losses might have to be cut. That means aims have to be rethought, relationships ended, new arrangements made. But one had better be confident that this is not merely running away or abandoning something that in reality still has life in it. Deciding to end a friendship, a marriage or a business partnership certainly might be the right thing to do, but only if one is clear and honest with oneself that doing so genuinely serves a good.

Actually most people make the opposite mistake, that is, they persist with relationships beyond the appropriate limit. That limit is reached when the harm, the toxic effect, of the relationship outweighs the good. When a relationship has become invested with resentments and refusals, when it depresses and prevents, makes for unhappiness, feeds on frictions, it has either to be spring-cleaned or abandoned. Life really is too short – less than a thousand months long, to repeat and repeat – to delay grasping the chance of being involved in making it good to be alive for oneself and different others, others with whom one has a better chance of being a better person, and able to give and to do better things.

The note of endeavour and achievement should also seem obvious as a component of what yields meaning, but two related points are worth mentioning in connection with it. The first is best illustrated by a remark that one of John F. Kennedy's speech-writers supplied for a famous speech that Kennedy made at the Rice Stadium on 12 September 1962, in which he declared the United States' intention of putting a man on the moon before the end of that decade. 'We choose to go to the moon in this decade and do the other things, not because they are easy, but because they are hard, because that goal will serve to organise and measure the best of our energies and skills,' Kennedy said, expressing a sentiment that has become, in so many respects, strangely unfashionable in a world of quick technologised ease. It is perhaps a rather Victorian sentiment, this idea that we do things because they are testing and tests make us grow, but the Victorians were not wrong about everything, and in particular they were not wrong about this.

There is an allied truth, that submitting oneself to the challenge and disagreement of others is another constructive experience. Why would one wish to escape opportunities to make advances in the things that concern us, if they come through accepting challenges like that? Answer: timidity, a dislike of embarrassment, fear of failure or ridicule, anxiety about being conspicuous. Some contemporary cultures have an aversion to anything that, or anyone who, stands out from the flock, partly in reaction to the artificial distinctions of class that once organised society to its detriment. But these reasons are not good ones for shrinking to the back of the crowd, for not risking the chance of learning something by being disagreed with or proved wrong.

Anyway, the point about endeavour and achievement is mainly about endeavour – about getting stuck in, in other words; welcoming the opportunity to do hard things, and experiencing the immense gratification of achievement when success attends. In the nature of the case success often enough does not attend, but that is another opportunity – it is itself one of the hard things that make for advancement.

The second point worth mentioning is that the endeavour of life does well – arguably, does best – if it involves a lifelong commitment to education. That does not mean evening classes and the like, necessarily; the best education is responsive and reflective reading, with discussion as a major adjunct if one can find *interlocuteurs valables*. It definitely means remaining alert, open, questioning, gathering information and superinducing order upon it, finding out, not resting content with half-answers and vague suppositions. Everyone knows that there is an awful lot of rubbish in circulation, so healthy scepticism is a requisite; and at the same time there is an awful lot of snobbery, attached to a false idea that the only things worth knowing or listening to are novelties. Wisdom and truth are not the preserve of the latest fashion, though some think so.

The worst mistake societies make is to think that education belongs to the years between the ages of five and sixteen or twenty-one. In the Basle of the great Jacob Burckhardt, historian of the Renaissance, the regents of the city's university required that its professors should teach not only their pupils but the whole community. That is a noble idea;

nobler still is the assumption thereby made that the whole community would wish to have a lifelong opportunity to learn, as a natural part of intelligent citizenship and – still more – observance of Aristotle's dictum that 'We educate ourselves to make noble use of our leisure.' Add the thought that one should naturally wish to be an intelligent citizen of the world, and to make best use of all one's gifts and opportunities, and the point makes itself.

And to repeat: the best education is found in responsive reading and discussion. There are many distractions available in our world to diminish the appetite for both, and mainly the former; but although there are distractions, there are no excuses.

That, by a not too unobvious path, seamlessly introduces the note of truth. Here two things might be said, among the many worth being thought. One is that the phrase 'being true', etymologically derived from the idea of straightness, as in the flight of an arrow true to the mark, at least implies directness, honesty in emotion and thought, confrontation with and acceptance of fact, lack of evasion and obfuscation, and refusal to escape into pieties, nostrums, or comforting delusions, especially self-delusions. It implies facing up to the world as it is, even if doing so is preface to trying to change the world into what one wishes it to be. It implies listening and hearing what others say about oneself, and judging squarely whether they have a point. In sum, it implies clear eyes and courageous acceptance of what is the case all round.

These remarks relate to honesty of living. Living honestly is hard to do, and it must be acknowledged that few of us are fully capable of it. We all delude ourselves sometimes about some things, hide from awkward facts, disguise our feelings, create little fabrics of helpful lies for ourselves and for people we care about, refuse to accept that the world or other people are as they all too obviously seem, and much besides. These are part of the strategy of living, a way of coping with the sharp angles and hard corners of life. It is perfectly understandable, and in enough cases even commendable – when it is kindly meant, to spare others' feelings or to patch over difficulties.

And some might think that a wholly honest world would be a stark place, and even a less interesting one. Perhaps. But the effort to sound the note of truth in the respects mentioned is unarguably right, as a component of a life intended to be good. The accumulation of little dishonesties and prevarications in one's feelings and dealings, and in one's facing up to the world, eventually make one feel sullied, even defeated, because they are all in the end evasions, and at some level we know it.

A powerful way of making the point about living truthfully in this sense is to say that we should be able to give a robust response to criticism of the way we live, where the criticism is not merely the challenge posed by those who disagree with or dislike us, but by our own reflective knowledge. By this latter is meant everything is garnered from experience, from interaction with others, from thoughtful reading and honest debating.

The importance of the sense of process in this arises from the fact that questions of value differ from questions of fact in that whereas the latter, in the ideal, are objective because independent of the choices, preferences, needs and desires of individuals, the former are not. Our moral concerns are shaped by our character and circumstances, and by our emotions – and to a significant extent by luck (where and when we were born, and into what conditions; whom we meet, what happens in the world around us – and much besides). In this setting we require to do our best in ensuring that what we learn is as accurate as possible, and that we and others are sincere in the majority of our dealings.

In fact, the idea of truth in living might better be described as sincerity, or even authenticity – this latter not quite in the sense, made familiar in philosophical discussion, of refusing to live by others' choices, although the idea is allied, but rather in the sense of seeking to stand square both to the world and to one's responsibly chosen aims. This could not happen if there were something wrong either with one's angle to the world or the defensibility of one's aims against good challenge. In the end, the idea of truth in the construction of good lives is the idea of straightness in orientation to both those things.

The note of freedom is the note of independence of thought, of autonomy, of the ultimate responsibility of a human agent for his or her choices. This note was sounded most loudly, for our purposes, in two chapters of the same story in the liberation of the human spirit: in classical antiquity, especially in that Athenian moment when thought took wing, and in the eighteenth-century Enlightenment, the core of which was its claim to the autonomy of the individual. In one sense it is a speaking indictment of the centuries that lay between the assertion and the reassertion of this freedom that the latter was necessary at all. Of course in neither case was the freedom absolute: Socrates was given the choice of exile or hemlock – he famously chose the latter – for corrupting the youth of Athens, and both Hume and Gibbon had to drape a veil, admittedly very diaphanous, over their atheism. But at the long worst point of the intervening two thousand years it was death to think differently from authority, let alone act in ways that it proscribed.

There is a vexed question in metaphysics about freedom of the will. At its crudest the question is whether there is such a thing as moral agency, or whether causality in nature makes everything that happens, including the activities of human beings, the outcome of antecedent causes, which in their turn are the effects of yet earlier causes, and so on indefinitely back – the implication being that what we do is not the result of genuinely free choices and decisions, but the ineluctable force of causality sweeping through us from the backward abysm of history. There are strong arguments on all sides of the debate, of which there are at least three main ones, one saying that there is freedom, one saying that there is none, and one saying that freedom of the will and causal determinism are compatible.

That is not a debate for here, because here the assumption has to be that human beings are genuine agents, that is, are genuinely capable of agency in the full meaning of being able to make choices and to act upon them in ways that introduce novelty into the order of things. This assumption grants that upbringing, social constraints, and natural limitations and inhibitions, all conspire to make the agent rather unfree in obvious ways. But this lack of freedom is a contingent matter; if differently placed, in different societies or none, the agent would not be constrained in those ways. In any case, he could act against the constraints if he dared, though it might be unwise or dangerous to do so. This way with matters reflects the thought that the concept of freedom lies at the root of the very possibility of ethical life – itself a compound of the concepts in particular of free choice and action, in the sense that ultimately no one else is responsible for an agent's choices of values and aims, nor for the acts that follow from those choices. Without this assumption as the starting point, all talk of ethics is empty.

A quick way to see why is to recognise that if what people do was inscribed in causal antecedents millions of years ago, and has come to pass because of the undeviating flow of causality ever since, praising or blaming them for what happens is futile. They do not act, but are acted upon; they are not agents, but patients of an involuntary process.

In leaving aside the metaphysical question of freedom and determinism, therefore, we are acknowledging reliance on a profound assumption: that here by 'freedom' is meant, in full awareness of the (so to speak) metaphysical risk, the contingently limited but real freedom of agency required for the very notion of ethics to make sense.

Most people who lived in Athens of the classical period were (contingently) very unfree; they were slaves, women, and children, and only adult male citizens were enfranchised. But the reason why Athens is nevertheless regarded as providing the first chapter in the story of freedom – specifically, freedom of the mind – is that the enfranchised were able to discuss, enquire, challenge and argue without having to pay lip-service to orthodoxies. It was this feature that Kant fastened upon in defining Enlightenment, not as a state but as a process of asserting independence of thought. In his celebrated essay 'What is Enlightenment?' he wrote:

> Enlightenment is man's emergence from his self-imposed immaturity. Immaturity is the inability to use one's understanding without guidance from another. This immaturity is self-imposed when its cause lies not in lack of understanding, but in lack of resolve and courage to use it without guidance from another. Sapere Aude! (dare to know) – 'Have courage to use your own understanding!' – that is the motto of enlightenment.

And then he struck the note of freedom fully:

> Nothing is required for enlightenment except freedom; and the freedom in question is the least harmful of all, namely,

the freedom to use reason publicly in all matters. But on all sides I hear: 'Do not argue!' The officer says, 'Do not argue, drill!' The tax man says, 'Do not argue, pay!' The pastor says, 'Do not argue, believe!'

The message is clear enough: thinking for oneself is one of the essentials of a good life because what issues from doing so is one's own. If others, or orthodoxies of some kind, do one's thinking for one, nothing is one's own. The life well lived is not any form of servitude, except as service to one's aims and loves. Thus is freedom central to meaning, as meaning is central to the good life.

It is surely unnecessary to say much about the note of beauty. It would be hard to argue that a life is as good as it might be if it is unrelievedly flat, grey and boring, without ornament or grace notes, without visual texture, harmonious sounds, vistas, the creations of human ingenuity and wit, colour and line, dance, flowers – in short, the amenities that please the senses and the intelligence, decorate the lived environment, and thereby yield emotional refreshment. These are among the things that beauty does, leaving aside the differences of taste which raise questions about beauty's status in the world – whether objective or wholly subjective, though if the latter it is surprising how much agreement there is about it.

Almost every home – at least, in parts of the world whose denizens are not enslaved to the basic necessities of finding water and food – has pictures and ornaments in it, a variety of colours in the furniture and decoration, and often the means of making music. These are practical proofs of the place that beauty holds among human needs above the basics. Art is not invariably or even perhaps mainly about beauty, but often enough embodies or celebrates it. Natural beauty is unfailing in its attraction to the human spirit, and we seek it out endlessly, yearning pleasantly for what it gives. The ubiquity of beautifications – think of body art and carefully cultivated gardens – is mark enough of the more general desire for it. There are good reasons that empirical psychology can give for the place it occupies in human consciousness, but as a commonplace of experience it scarcely needs science to iterate the point. So perhaps the only requirement is to offer a reminder that the quality of the setting in which life is lived far more often than not affects the quality of the life thus lived.

Seeing familiar points applied in different settings typically reinforces them. While living in the Far East, in China and later Japan, I was much struck by the ethical importance attached to objects of vertu, to ornamental gardens, to ponds and vistas, to admired calligraphy and ink drawings, to poems, to individuality in the simplest things such as a blossom, an insect, the curves of a tree's branches. The remarkable ability to enjoy such things in these two otherwise very different cultures bears out Walter Pater's telling remark that 'It is only the dullness of the eye that makes any two things seem alike,' and helps one appreciate the writings of such as Junichiro Tanizaki (many others from these absorbing traditions could be cited), whose *In Praise of Shadows* is a hymn to aesthetics in the good life. In it he talks of the pleasure of heaving wind among bamboo leaves, of raindrops after a shower dropping on moss around the foot of a stone lantern, of subdued light playing on lacquerware. The point about seeking out and enjoying the beauty in things is, as this shows, the mindfulness involved, an alertness to the good to be found everywhere even among the ordinary.

Doubtless this smacks of a certain preciosity, and so it might seem to pragmatic sensibilities; but it is hard to imagine even these latter as wholly immune to the emotional impact of beauty – although they might be more moved by things sublime, majestic, and spectacular. And why not? The important thing is to be, so to say, movable by beauty. It is paralleled by our capacity to be moved by novels and films – moved to sympathy or fear, exercising our capacities for the kind of responses that make us full members of the moral community, able at our best to understand others and to communicate with them on better than superficial terms. Anything that educates our sensibilities has this tendency, and is therefore indispensable to constructing the good. Encountering beauty and recognising it as such calls deeply on our sensibilities and responses, and that is what makes it one of the central components of a sense of life's worth.

The note of fulfilment, simply, is the integration of all the foregoing into a conscious project of trying to live well and flourishingly. It would be unnecessary to single out this note as a factor were it not for the fact that a commonplace of living, especially in our distracted and fragmented contemporary lives, is that unity of purpose is often exactly what is missing; yet without it the other notes do not sound together, and do not constitute a whole that is distinctively one's own.

One good sense of the term 'integrity' denotes honesty and consistency of principle; but another, not unrelated, sense denotes the considered fitting together of elements of a person's character and purposes, in ways that are mutually supportive and enhancing. For Aristotle, the person who uses his practical wisdom (*phronesis*) to judge the best route through life, avoiding extremes and therefore achieving virtue (as the mean between extremes; thus courage is the middle way between rashness and cowardice, generosity is the middle way between meanness and profligacy), exemplifies this integration of thought and action. His critics say that the philosophy of the middle way is too middle brow, middle class and middle aged, and they have a point; extremes – of ecstasy, passion, delight – ought not to be omitted from the repertoire. But he also has a point for the pursuit of the good in the ordinary avocations of practical life, when the heights and depths are not to the point.

And so the idea of integration of all aspects of one's striving for the good, of harmony between them, of balance, mutuality, and fittingness, accords with some of the most ancient precepts about the life worth living; as for example also in the thought of Plato, for whom the idea of harmony or integration is fundamental. For him, achievement of it is the goal of the quest, and is what fulfilment means.

In other moralities, notably traditional ones associated with religions, the keynote is obedience to a set of injunctions, submission to a vastly powerful will that has long ago issued its demands and has promised rewards and punishments accordingly. In the humanistic conception sketched here, the good life is individually something chosen and built, and this autonomy is its distinctive mark. But it is not individualistic in a negative sense; it is not a form of ethical egoism, because it rests so firmly on the idea that good relationships are essential to it, and on the idea that one's own fulfilments cannot be complete in tandem with consciousness of barriers to the chance of fulfilment for others. One of our duties to ourselves is to feel our duties to others; and to live them.

CHAPTER 3

When Darkness Falls

Hercules' mother was Alcmene, one of many mortal woman who were variously seduced or raped by Zeus, king of the gods, and bore his children as a result – in this activity Zeus was following the precedent of other gods in the legends of the world, legends that anticipate a version of the tale which, for reasons too many and diverse to permit discussion here, has been taken literally by some in the course of the last two millennia.

As with others of Zeus' amours, his tryst with Alcmene provoked the jealousy of Hera. Accordingly she persecuted Alcmene's son Hercules in frightful ways. Her worst assult on him was the infliction of an attack of delusional insanity that made him kill his beloved wife Megara and their children. It was in atonement for this – note the curious logic of the Greek mythology: the deed was not his fault, but it was he who paid – that he had to submit himself to the will of King Eurystheus and carry out the labours for which he is chiefly known.

Reflecting on a quite different myth – an Old Testament one, of the chaste and self-contained wife of Potiphar who was suddenly stricken with love for Joseph of the many-coloured coat – Thomas Mann realised that such stories perennially attracted him because of a truth they convey, a truth about the fragility of the order we try to impose on life, and the danger of disruption that always threatens it from unexpected quarters. He wrote in his notebooks that his works always recurred in different ways to the same idea,

> the idea of catastrophe, the invasion of destructive and wanton forces into an ordered scheme and a life bent upon self-control and happiness conditioned by it. The saga of peace wrung from conflict and seemingly assured; of life laughingly sweeping away the structure of art; of mastery and overpowering, and the coming [into it] of the stranger god.

Allied to this was the sequel of such catastrophe if one survived it – the guilt or regret that stained the spirit, the hole torn in the fabric of things by loss and grief, the vertigo of near-madness, despair and pain that come from one or other of the derailments of hope.

Such was Hera's savage revenge on Hercules for being the product of her husband's infidelity: a catastrophe, an invasion of destructive and wanton force. There are many kinds of catastrophe, but three seem especially like the irruption of a malign deity's will into one's endeavours – like an unfeeling hand striking down what, in the ensuing mess, suddenly seems to have been no more than a precarious and painstakingly balanced house of cards – and they are: the loss of those we love, the suffering of injustice, and the purchase of guilt.

To live is to contract for loss. Only if you die before the deaths of people you care about, and never separate from any of them because of a quarrel or because they move away or abroad – in short: only if every one of the thousands of exit doors that take people out of each other's lives stay shut until your own opens out of all of theirs, will you not know loss of this kind. Your parents would have to live very long, and your friends also, as well as the people you do not know personally but whose presence and action in the world make a positive difference to you. They would have to stay alive and present, they would have to remain enough the same to be the people you do not wish to lose. Given the impossibilities connoted here, the original point holds: to live is to contract for loss.

One task of living is preparation for this possibility. At times the possibility will become fact, and in ways very hard to bear. Grief takes years to assuage – not to go away; we learn to live with it, not without it – and it comes back to visit even years after the event, even when the grief we feel is for someone lost through divorce or a final quarrel, though such loss cannot compare to the complete and shocking finality of the losses caused by death.

In the starkest, rawest moments of grief there seems no help other than what endurance can afford, and occasionally sleep; unless we remember to reflect on what the dead would wish for us in our grief – to take comfort in the fact that they would not want us to mourn too long or bitterly, but instead to remember the best of them, and the best of our time with them, and to live courageously with face turned to the world, in ways they would applaud if they could know of them.

One of the keenest of pains comes from suffering injustice. We all suffer injustice, in lesser and greater ways. Emerson said we should give others the least of what we give a painting, namely, the advantage of a good light; but that happens insufficiently often to make the world seem a fair place. It is not a fair place; it is full of actual and egregious injustice. One stockbroker earns in a year what dozens of hospital nurses between them do. A teenaged pop idol can make more in a couple of years than most individuals in the world make in a lifetime. Top football players in Britain are paid in a week what it takes the average British worker ten years to earn. And so on. No: the world is not a fair place, and largely for the reason that it is not a rational one. The value placed on pop music and football as against that placed on a hospital nurse or a teacher is out of all reason disproportionate to real value. In such a world small and big injustices are commonplace; they are the norm; they are therefore what we should expect – even from the law, that blunt, blundering instrument too heavy and broad to feel the nuances and special circumstances that it crushes down upon once it is summoned into motion.

Greed and folly, the unequal distribution of power, the profoundly inequitable starting places in the race of life, are the motors of injustice. And this is to say nothing yet about the injustices that flow like blood from a severed artery as a result of human rights violations, tyranny, war, and chaos, all prevalent in many parts of the world, where it is frankly better never to have been born than to live a single day.

This is old news, indeed it is such old news that people do not even think about it, if they can possibly help it; so long as the worst injustices are perpetrated against someone unknown far enough away, why care? And therefore much of it passes ignored.

For Thomas Mann guilt was a special category of what the 'stranger god' might inflict by shattering the frail bonds of our life constructions. He thought particularly of the amount of suffering that a sensitive conscience would feel as a result of doing wrong:

The barb of the bad conscience sharpens the moral sense.
It should not be thought that the guilty one is immoral,
quite the opposite ... Only the thick-witted should commit

crimes; they do not mind, they live from day to day and nothing worries them. Evil is for the dull-witted; anyone with traces of sensibility should avoid it if he possibly can, for he will have to smart for it. That he has a conscience makes him worse off than ever; he will be punished precisely on account of his conscience.

And from this insight Mann developed one of his central themes: that guilt drives men to spiritual development, to elevation of heart and mind prompted by the desire to overcome the old Adam and substitute the new.

The alternative is a form of inner crippling, having to take the dead weight of remorse and self-accusation everywhere, corrupting relationships and possibilities, stunting growth. The message is not that one should seek occasions for guilt in the hope that repair will lead to greater things; but that if this particular form of darkness falls, the way to go is towards the light.

Loss, grief, injustice, guilt: to this list, if it were not litany enough, might be added illness, poverty, failure, disappointment, rejection, despair, depression, and all the other possibilities of the debit side of life, many and familiar, which are the common lot of humankind. Even among the lucky people who live in rich and largely peaceful parts of the world these things can seem so bad that they prompt thoughts, and sometimes the actuality, of suicide, or at the very least dark nights of the soul and deep suffering. Perhaps they are in fact more common in the rich and peaceful places; in parts of the world far less happily placed, the struggle for survival, or the very simplicity of the things that afford relief and pleasure, might paradoxically mean that people there are better off in these intangible respects than their materially more fortunate brethren.

Obviously enough, people struggling to find clean water to drink and enough food to eat have little opportunity or, indeed, reason to suffer the kind of anxieties and ills, often self-induced, of life in the developed world. But it is also the case that their chance for flourishing and creative lives is much circumscribed by the hard struggle for life's basics. And they constitute the world's majority. In his 'Elegy' Thomas Gray mourned the silence of those never given a chance to speak, the lost genius and unsung poetry of human beings submerged in ignorance, poverty and lack of opportunity by the grind of bare existence.

In both senses of 'this goes without saying', all this goes without saying. And as already suggested, it places a demand on everyone with the means to make a difference in some way to improving the chances of those with little chance. Humanity is in fact a fellowship, and ought to be more of one in practice. But it is in lives and places where people have a chance to reflect, choose and act that the demands of a good life – the life worth living – come most sharply into focus, and the endeavour cannot be stalled by the thought that not enough people yet have that chance. Whenever the chance exists, the place for thought about grief, failure, guilt, illness, and the other vicissitudes, exists likewise, as what has to be taken into account in the construction of the good. For 'the stranger god' is too apt to enter, not least when all seems well.

When darkness falls, the first demand in response is for courage, the second is for patience, the third is for endurance. Time really does heal what death does not heal, though this fact is very little consolation in the darkest part of the dark. Knowing how little comfort there is in such times should make us more conscious of the agony and isolation of others travelling the dark stretches; and might prompt us to offer them the one thing that brings a small touch of light, like the glimmer of a firefly, into that night – which is one's company and kindness, if sensitively given.

PART II
Practical Morality

CHAPTER 4

Attitudes and the Great Questions

What distinguishes the Hercules story among all the legends of gods and heroes is this hero's mighty twelve labours, undertaken in expiation of the horrendous crime that Hera made him commit – which was, recall, the murder of his wife and children in a lunatic frenzy. Why twelve labours? One suggestion is that because there are twelve metopes on the Temple of Zeus at Olympia, and the labours were chosen as the illustration for them, they had to fit that number. A better explanation is that twelve in a significant number in the arithmetic of practical life; the reason why in our own living memory there were twelve pennies in a shilling is that this allows more ways of dividing shillings easily into coins of various smaller component denominations than a decimal system.

The number matters less than the fact that in expiation for the crime Hera made him commit, Hercules had to undertake perilous and onerous tasks: killing dangerous beasts – a lion, a many-headed snake, a flock of vicious birds – fetching precious or very hard-to-get objects from difficult places, cleaning away a vast amount of filth, and more (read Apollodorus for the original story of Hercules' mighty labours). The tale of course symbolises a variety of things;

for our purposes what matters is its reminder that living is doing, and that doing involves choosing, adopting attitudes and premising one's actions upon them, sometimes confronting the hard task of dealing with dilemmas. And this takes place in the arena of ordinary life. In this second part I canvass some questions of moral practicality of the kind our contemporary world exemplifies. To set the scene for this change of gear in our discussion, a preamble is required.

In thinking about anything that has either a moral dimension or implications of a moral kind, there is a close relationship between saying how things are and how things should be – at the very least because when one describes how things are, one is immediately tempted to add either 'and so they should be' or 'they should be otherwise'; for moral consideration is not a neutral matter, but concerns the realm of action, choice, and the character of life, where bare description is never enough.

Given the difficulties, how is one to learn how to make good judgements about morally sensitive matters? One contribution might come from a knowledge of history, a rich source of instruction for anyone who investigates it attentively. Even here, though, the derivable lessons can often be too general, too ambiguous, and sometimes contradictory. Moral history can seem endlessly cyclical, with periods of austerity succeeding relative liberalism, which in turn liberalise after a time, only to retrench again. Sometimes there seems to be an inertia in human affairs, reversing progress at every opportunity of war or disaster.

Perhaps, though, such remarks are tendentious; history, including moral history, never exactly repeats itself; and nothing is ever quite lost from the argument of time. Moreover there is always a danger of our reading present value-judgements back into the record; for example, commentators used to say that, in its successful republican youth, Rome was austere and chaste, and that the voluptuousness of its later imperial stages was a symptom of decline. When we do this, history cannot teach us much, for it is (absurdly) being made to take lessons from our present.

But there is indeed something to be learned from the history of morality. It is that it consists in a struggle – a Heraclitean one, as the flux back and forth shows, and a Herculean one, given how much of the happiness of mankind is at stake – between what, for brevity, one might call 'liberal' and 'conservative' values. I speak of the history of the Western world – the world of essentially European and Judaeo-Christian origin. The only safe comment about our moral fate in this tradition is that it inevitably involves struggle, with no real ascendancy between either party, but with each thinking that the other is ascendant – and occasionally, to the real distress of the other, with one of them temporarily being so. Most people, as individuals, never belong fully to either party, but hover between, tending to err on the liberal side in respect of their own conduct and on the conservative side in respect of others' conduct. One large difference between the parties is that when the conservatives have the upper hand they actively persecute the liberals (in the past going so far as to burn them at the stake), whereas the liberals, when ascendant, cause conservatives no greater agonies than those of disapproval and chagrin.

But there is something else to be said about our moral fate, the most important thing of all. This is that it is not fixed or predestined; it is our own to make. The nature of morality turns on what we choose it to be. It is not there, laid like railway tracks running from the past onwards into time, for us helplessly to trundle along, surprised or dismayed by what comes into view. As masters of our destiny, we have a duty to think as clearly as we can about what kind of people we wish to be and what kind of life we wish to lead; and then to choose, and to act, as wisely as we are able.

As a contribution to choosing the right attitudes in these vital matters – 'The meaning of things lies not in things themselves, but in our attitudes to them,' said Antoine de Saint-Exupéry – what follows sets out both the conservative and liberal views. But it does so tendentiously, for it is firmly on the side of the latter, for – to repeat – morality is not a neutral matter. Accordingly the following sections are written in polemical and somewhat prescriptive mode, for this is an essay in moralising, not in moral philosophy. It is also brief, and therefore summary; the questions it addresses are complicated and delicate, and have been, and continue to be, discussed in the wider debate that society has with itself in many different forums, from academic seminars to newspaper columns and beyond. As a contribution to that debate, the following remarks presuppose it; but they also constitute an argument for a change of perspective, which if accepted would help to change the debate's terms.

The difference between moral philosophy and moralising merits comment. Some moral philosophers deny that it is their job to moralise – by which they mean: to offer guidance, and to say how one should choose and act – on the ground that they are no better fitted to do so than anyone else. Instead they see their task as clarification of the concepts used in moral debate (for chief examples: 'goodness', 'right', 'duty' and 'obligation'), together with investigation of the reasoning employed about them. Moral philosophy thus conceived is a neutral, purely descriptive task, which studiously avoids offering views about how to live.

This is a recent development. Past moral philosophers were concerned to identify and enjoin the good life, and to recommend ways of resolving the problems whose occurrence is guaranteed by the complexity of human existence. Given the three facts that life is a demanding business, that many search for guidance in how to live it, and that most who offer to guide them do so from partisan religious or political standpoints, it seems not just a pity, but a dereliction, that moral philosophy has turned its back on the task; for philosophy is the enterprise of reason, which tries to take the large, clear view, guided by logic and the facts – from which, therefore, one might reasonably hope for more judicious results than partisan faiths or factions can offer.

In any case, moralising needs moral philosophy. In moralising one has to reason from principles, which in turn require grounds. Although what I argue here is an act of moralising, it therefore also includes at least something of its justification.

Most of what I say in this part will be regarded as mere common sense by some, and as highly controversial by others. Past example shows that it is hard to persuade the latter to think and behave differently; but the argument with them must be continued nevertheless, for their views remain influential – and, arguably, harmful.

To most people, discussion of morality suggests discussion of a familiar range of topics: the family, sex, drugs, crime; the implications of medical advances; standards in public life. But this perception of what matters most is not universal. It is chiefly believed in the Anglo-Saxon West, in Muslim countries and in China. This geo-social remark is intended to give pause, as reminding us that in (for example) non-Anglo-Saxon Europe, especially northern Europe, not all of the problems listed, least of all sex and drugs, seem quite so acute; not because people there indulge less in either, but because they are more tolerant of both. A comparative study of moral attitudes in the world's societies would indeed be instructive, among other things showing that one reason why North America and Britain differ from continental Europe in the noted respect is that more austere, less tolerant varieties of Protestant Christianity have been influential there. It might also show that where Christian or Muslim missionaries have not penetrated, the peoples of Africa, South America and the Pacific Islands perceive the moral realm differently – as they still do in India, and once did in pre-Communist China.

These generalisations admittedly verge on over-generalisations, but they serve the purpose of keeping before us the thought that moralities are socially constructed and historically shaped. It is healthy to remember that what is taboo or acceptable in one culture might be the reverse in another. At very least, that fact should make one keenly re-examine one's own values.

The great moral questions – the most important and urgent ones – are not about sex, drugs, and unmarried mothers. They are, instead, about human rights, war and genocide, the arms trade, poverty in the Third World, the continuance of slavery under many guises and names, interreligious antipathies and conflicts, and inequality and injustice everywhere. These areas of concern involve truly staggering horrors and human suffering. In comparison to them, the parochial and largely misguided anxieties over sex, drugs, gay marriage, and the other matters that fill newspapers and agitate the 'Moral Majority' in America and Britain, pale into triviality. It is itself a moral scandal that these questions preoccupy debate in comfortable corners of the world, while real atrocity and oppression exist elsewhere.

This is not to deny that some of the parochial concerns are important, for they are; and there are also genuinely significant concerns such as gay rights in general, stem-cell research, abortion, and the implications for medical practice and humanity's future in the revolution in genetic science. But as I shall argue later, their importance lies in what is almost invariably the opposite of what moral conservatives think.

There is also the ethical challenge posed by environmental problems caused by the heedless and insatiable rush for economic growth everywhere – in the developing world where standards of pollution control are poor, and in the developed world where gargantuan energy consumption is poisoning and degrading the air we breathe and the water we drink, the soil that grows our crops and the weather that keeps the world in equilibrium. Failing to grow wiser even by an inch or two in this arena makes all other debates otiose, for we shall not be here to need them.

The claim that human rights violations, war and Third World poverty are the greatest of moral problems hardly needs explanation or justification. The piteous agonies of refugees, the starving, the massacred, the tortured, the imprisoned, are eloquent in their own case. It is astonishing how many in the world's comfortable regions are nightly able to witness the plight of their fellow humans, only to turn off their television sets and forget what they saw. Perhaps the reason is that individuals feel helpless in the face of so much and such profound suffering. Beyond making a donation to a suitable charity – and there is a reasonable limit to what one can give – the next step in active concern threatens to consume too much of one's time and resources, thereby disrupting one's own projects in life.

This suggests that it is better for governments to take action, as the collective agency of the people they serve. Impelled by their electorates, they could, and on this view should, act in concert to halt those among their number who violate their citizens' rights, or make war. And yet, look where an admittedly poor analogue of this sentiment in favour of intervention and pre-emption has landed the world. Where there was a hole, everyone kept on digging, contrary to the sage advice that holes of that kind are precisely where one stops digging.

The United Nations organisation embodies a noble aspiration to the end of keeping peace or restoring it in troubled parts of the world; but in practice it is enfeebled by its members' divisions and its lack of funds, so that the good it does is limited. But it still does good at times, not least in representing ideals – among which the Universal Declaration of Human Rights is central.

When the UN came into existence at the end of the Second World War one of its earliest acts was to respond to the appalling atrocities of the preceding years by boldly committing itself to the ideal of treating every human individual in the world as possessed of basic rights, and of trying to protect those rights. The Charter of the UN, adopted in 1945, affirmed 'faith in fundamental human rights, in the dignity and worth of the person, and in the equal rights of men and women and of nations large and small'. Accordingly the UN established a committee to draft a Universal Declaration. The committee worked swiftly despite a few pauses over disagreements (mainly from Stalin's Soviet Russia not wishing interference in its internal affairs: no need to wonder why), and the Declaration was adopted in 1948 without a dissenting vote. At the time it was particularly welcomed by Third World countries and subjects of colonial rule. Since then the Universal Declaration has been supplemented by two Covenants, respectively on political and civil rights and on social and economic rights, which along with further instruments and agreements together constitute an International Bill of Human Rights.

It might seem that these resolutions, these high-sounding documents and covenants, have little practical worth, because human rights violations continue everywhere in the world, often in the grossest forms. Yet their mere existence changes the terms of international debate, and gives powerful aid to individuals and groups opposing violations of them – witness the patient endeavours of non-governmental organisations in campaigning on human rights issues. Progress is slow – painfully so, usually – but the existence of an International Bill of Human Rights and of its use by NGOs and governments represents a striking historical departure. One of its chief effects is felt in international legal proceedings, surely one of the most optimistic signs for the world's future.

The Universal Declaration is a bold document. It starts from the claim that 'all members of the human family' enjoy 'inherent dignity and equal and inalienable rights' and that upon the recognition of this rests our best hopes of achieving the great universal desiderata of freedom, justice, and peace. Disregard for these rights led to the barbarities of the Second World War, vivid in the memory of the international community, which, as it emerged from their shadow, sought to renew its hopes for 'a world in which human beings shall enjoy freedom of speech and belief and freedom from fear and want'. Recognising that such aspirations merit the protection of law, the UN's Declaration sets out to describe what that law should encompass. The chief provisions are that all human beings are born free and equal in rights, and that these latter include life, liberty, and security, freedom from slavery and cruel punishment, recognition before and protection by law, freedom of movement, freedom to have and express views, to participate in the government of the state, to have an education, to own property, to have time for leisure, to make choices in personal life, and to enjoy peace. Correlatively, the Declaration recognises that everyone has duties to others and to the community, which in sum make it possible for others to enjoy the same rights also.

These principles by now seem commonplace to people in the West, for whom they state a mere minimum of expectation. But to the majority of the world's population they are still ideals rather than realities, and for anyone languishing in political detention, or in the shadow of a harsh regime, they represent precious aspirations. Philosophical discussion of the basis and justification of rights continues; but one could abbreviate it by *laying claim* to those rights, defending one's arrogation of them on the ground that history – experience – has taught us what best promotes human flourishing, and that enjoyment of these rights is essential to it.

One main purpose of ethics might be to help people see that human rights abuses are chief among the moral problems facing the world, and to urge them to act accordingly. People need only decide to do something about the problems thus identified; at the very least to write, and to keep on writing, to their political representatives, demanding collective action; and voting accordingly – and never forgetting that the truly important moral questions lie here. If there is an arena where the greatest challenges for the future lie, and with them therefore the greatest need for moral heroism and endeavour, it is in this sphere. The development of science and technology shows us that, as a species, we have grown clever; their misuse for war and oppression shows us that we have not yet grown wise. Moral heroism is required for us to teach ourselves wisdom.

I shall say more about the great question of human rights later, for two reasons. The first is that a debate about the interpretation of the aspirations embodied in human rights documents is required, in order to show what they can and should mean in practice. For example, the right to life is not a right to a mere existence, but to life of a certain quality and significance for the person living it. From this obvious-seeming fact a number of important considerations follow. One is that the 'right to life' entails a right to die – specifically a right to die in a manner and at a time of one's own choosing, and with the help of medical technology, if necessary, to make it a good and easeful death. Why does this follow? Because dying is a living act, something that happens in the course of life; and a right to life of a certain quality entails that dying should not be painful and terrifying if it can be made otherwise.

This unexpected-seeming result shows that the rights that humanity has properly and boldly claimed for itself are richer in meaning even than the first debates about them envisaged, and those richer meanings need to be drawn out as part of the philosophical and prudential framework for their application to real life and real people.

The second reason for recurring to the question of human rights is that our best chance of a global ethics lies with them, a global ethics to which all peoples, traditions, creeds, and ethnicities can subscribe. In one good sense the world's peoples already notionally agree that what is embodied in the International Bill of Human Rights serves as the basis of such an ethics; but alas, the self-interest of governments, or more accurately the politicians in charge of them, makes too many international actors resile from treating internationally shared human rights norms as binding on them. A distinguished Chinese scholar helped to draft the UN Declaration of Human Rights under the chairwomanship of Mrs Roosevelt in the late 1940s; today's China claims that the concept of human rights is an imposition on the rest of the world by successors of the European Enlightenment, implying that human rights are not universal and that different traditions have different standards. This is nonsense on stilts, but it is shared by too many, including some Muslim theocrats who do not wish to accept what the International Bill of Rights says about women. So there is still a fight to be fought in generalising the possession, exercise, and defence of human rights to everyone in the world.

CHAPTER 5

Moral Attitudes and Ethics

I turn now to treat of some of the standard, familiar and more parochial problems in moral debate, involving what are seen at the individual level as threats to 'family values' and allied concerns, which for most people, as noted, turn on questions about marriage and divorce, sexual practices and behaviour, drug abuse, and such dilemmas as abortion and euthanasia. This list is not exhaustive, but it covers central ground.

It helps to recognise a distinction between narrow definitions of 'morality' as conceived in modern times (chiefly since the eighteenth century) and a more inclusive classical conception of 'ethics'. As the notion now operates, morality applies just to parts of life, chiefly to interpersonal relationships; and it invariably concerns such matters as marital infidelity and malicious gossip, telling lies, and being unkind. No one thinks that eating bananas is a moral matter, nor how a person works, nor what colour he paints his house. The philosophers of classical antiquity thought differently. For them all of life is an ethical matter: one lives and does well as a whole person, and both one's flourishing and effect on others flow from one's total character. For this reason life has to be considered – 'The unconsidered life,' said Socrates, 'is not worth living' – and it can be considered only if it is informed.

Questions about ethics, therefore, as against those having to do with more narrowly conceived morality, are questions about intelligent human flourishing – which is to say: human well-being and well-doing. They therefore seek answers not only to questions about what sort of people we should be, but about what sort of society we should have – so that the best we can aspire to be can have the best environment to thrive in. Thus ethics and politics, as Aristotle saw, are continuous.

Grasping the distinction between morality and ethics is important because it helps us to promote the latter. Morality is about what is allowed and forbidden in particular realms of behaviour; ethics is about the character of one's personality and life, and what flows from both in the way of choices, relationships and action. Therefore the groundwork of ethics is not rules and codes, admonitions and sanctions, as in morality, but an education of character whose primary target is the inculcation of thoughtfulness, insight, taste, and tolerance. The admittedly utopian conviction thus embodied is that from success in such an enterprise ethical society will grow; and in such a society the permissions and prohibitions with which morality concerns itself will be unnecessary because already comprised in the mutual respect and tolerance constituting the relationships among its members.

I turn to these larger considerations later. The best way of showing why they are worth promoting is to work through the main moral (in the narrow sense) debates that bedevil Western societies. Discussing them shows that the moral problems we think we face change character when viewed from what in the end is seen as an ethical perspective.

Most people are capable at times of being well judging and careful, and capable likewise of thinking things through in a generous frame of mind. In such moods one can recognise two facts, and two demands entailed by them, which are profoundly important to ethical considerations – and yet which are, as is often the case with profundities, simple.

The first fact is that we (for *any* 'we') have a good idea of what, in a general way, conduces to human flourishing. One can interpret the Universal Declaration of Human Rights as stating that understanding in full, but it can be put more summarily. Shelter, warmth, food, companionship, health, freedom, security: this is easily the list of desiderata which – irrespective of their historical or cultural setting – most people would acknowledge as among the necessary basics without which one cannot properly begin to construct a good life. Of course there is much more, of more complex and diverse kinds, that makes for full human flourishing, for humans are intelligent and creative animals; all the arts and sciences, and the various amenities of civilisation, show what we have found attractive besides.

The second fact might at first seem to conflict with the first. It is that there is a great variety of human interests, not all of which one can be confident of understanding. No one can see things from everyone else's point of view; few can expect to achieve real insight into the needs and desires of others merely on the basis of knowing their own. This is why George Bernard Shaw's amusing dictum, 'Do not do unto others as you would that they should do unto you. Their tastes may not be the same,' is actually a profound truth – for to think in the conventional way of 'Do to others what you would have them do to you' (far better is: 'Don't do to others what you would not have them do to you') is to make yourself the standard for others, to base your treatment of others on your personal outlook. Rather, in recognising and accepting the difference of others, sometimes the great difference from oneself, one is in a better position to understand what is appropriate in responding to them, in giving them space, in finding a way to share the world with them.

The conflict between the two facts is thus merely apparent. A relativist might dispute the first by saying that, if we think we know what people elsewhere or at other times regard as desirable, we risk misinterpreting them according to our own parochial views. But this argument is at best only half right, for the first fact is that we have a perfectly good general understanding of what makes for human flourishing, even if – as the second fact then adds – we have to learn more to discover what is sufficient for such flourishing on an individual basis, taking background differences and other considerations into account.

Two demands follow immediately from these two facts. The first is that if we know the least of what makes for the flourishing of others, then, if those others lack it – or are offered the opposite of it by, say, oppressors or natural disaster – this makes a call on us. To know that another is without the minimum that makes for human flourishing, and to ignore the fact, is wrong – or at very least, deeply imprudent; for, in a world in which people recognise others' needs but ignore them, one will oneself be sure to suffer as a result. Therefore, even on minimal prudential grounds, people do well to act in such a way that this is not a world in which we perceive but ignore each other's needs. (Below I give grounds for saying that it is not merely imprudent but unethical, in the inclusive classical sense, to act this way.)

The second demand is that, when we recognise the variety of human needs and desires, our first step must be to tolerate that variety, because it is so great that, as noted, we cannot always expect to have a ready insight into it; so the only way to avoid being mistaken, or prejudiced, or motivated by ignorance, is to be open-minded. Again the point can be substantiated by appeal even to the lowest motivation. We each wish to live our own lives and make our own choices, and in doing so to be respected or at least tolerated by others. We wish for sufficient latitude from others to carry out our own projects, even when they do not understand what our projects mean to us. Because we wish this to be a world where this happens, we have to extend the same consideration to others.

The generosity just premised rests, as noted, on the insight that we cannot expect to understand, without sympathy and the right kind of effort at least, people whose concerns are different from our own, especially if they inhabit other conditions or cultures. But this is not mere mindless tolerance; it is neither unqualified nor irrevocable. For there are intolerable acts – murder, rape, torture, oppression, terrorism, warmongering, and injustice – whose perpetrators, whoever they are, step absolutely beyond the pale. This again suggests the familiar 'harm principle': that whatever anyone does, he or she should be free to do it provided it does not harm others, and allows them to pursue their own goals under the same condition. This principle only says what one must not do – namely, that one must not interfere with or harm others (except in the very specific case of self-defence, and acting to prevent even greater harm). The first demand is stronger, having the form of a positive injunction: it says that we should help others when we recognise their need.

All this implies that the great sin is harm to people (which includes failing to help when one sees the need). One should say: the great sin is harm to other sentient creatures; but, although this is correct, I shall restrict discussion to humans here, for it is at least clear that they have a special place among sentient creatures, as having closer interests to our own, and as being capable of more various kinds of suffering.

I characterised the two demands at their lowest denominators, to show that even if we are merely self-regarding it is prudential to obey those demands. But of course I believe that we do far better with an ethics that adds other-regardingness to self-regardingness. This is done by recognising and respecting others' interests, so that by a thoughtful mutual navigation of concerns we always seek the best, and at times accept the least bad, for ourselves and each other, taken together. The justification is that living thus is more satisfying and fruitful for everyone concerned than if one met these demands merely out of self-interest; and the kind of world in which most people felt this way would be a better-quality world than one in which mere self-interest prompts us to tolerate, and occasionally to help, others when it is useful to ourselves to do so. For one would not always find it useful to help others; indeed, the imperatives of competition and advantage-seeking would often make it harmful to oneself to tolerate or help others; so such a world would only be patchily mutual at best – and, even then, for not very edifying reasons. It has to be admitted, alas, that this describes our world as it is.

These remarks touch on matters of importance in several further ways. They bear on a truth that gives much of the point to ethical and political debate, recognised as seamlessly connected. This is that in human communities both resources and sympathies are limited; that competition between individuals and groups is therefore inevitable, and can, and often does, lead to conflict; and that therefore we need laws, rules, and traditions to ameliorate our relationships, and to resolve conflicts. On the front line of these are ethical considerations, which enjoin a certain mutual attitude between people – of respect, consideration, and trust-keeping; of kindness where appropriate and fellowship where possible – and which constitute the reasons for a person's acting in one way rather than another when his or her actions affect others.

With these thoughts to hand, we can now turn to the standard questions of moral debate.

CHAPTER 6

'Family Values'

Most debate about morality clusters around a set of problems, or perceived problems, which are most easily identified by the proposed ideal with respect to which they are thought to fall short, namely, the morality of 'family values'. The concept of a model family and its behaviour is central to his view. That model is of a happy nuclear family of two parents, one of either sex, with obedient, well-socialised offspring, living together in the same household into which others come only by arrangement and temporarily. None of the family uses illegal drugs, and if they use legal ones (alcohol, nicotine) they do so moderately and sensibly. The parents limit their sexual interest to one another, and the offspring engage in sexual activity only when, as adults in their turn, they have committed themselves to a responsible relationship – standardly, a permanent monogamous marriage – with a member of the opposite sex. This family is economically independent, socially responsible, law-abiding, and observant of contemporary norms.

That is the minimum that a model 'family values' family should be. More evangelical supporters of this ethos urge families, in addition, to be against abortion, homosexuality, divorce, pornography, and too much welfarism (on the grounds that people should take responsibility for themselves), as well as in favour of hanging and other very severe punishments for crime. They also strongly oppose the use of drugs – some of them include the legal drugs too, as temperance and prohibition movements show. Many supporters of 'family values' justify all these views on religious grounds. (When they do, they also urge obedience to the prescriptions of the religion, and observance of its requirements and practices. This includes giving money to its organisation.)

This ethos is complex and interesting. Arguably, it is a mixture of something right and much wrong, the latter stemming from traditions of thought – again, principally religious – which are themselves complex.

What is right about this conservative ethos is that it recognises, and makes central, the value of settled domestic affections, by which I mean those that sustain long-term, committed, co-operative relationships based on affection and shared interests at the core of private life. Without doubt such affections, as found in the happiest marriages and most flourishing families, are a great good. It is scarcely needful to list their benefits. But such affections can be, and are, enjoyed in a large variety of ways, of which the 'family values' model family is only one, and – as its short history shows – a rather unsuccessful one. Moreover, the 'family values' school takes its attitudes to sex and sexuality, marriage and fertility, drugs, crime, and the nature of society, to be the corollary of their belief in the nuclear-family version of what promotes domestic affections. This, arguably, is a mistake – and sometimes a tragic one, as we can see from the number of social problems it causes. Conservative morality, in other words, is the problem, not the solution, in much that causes difficulty in society. This is because it is repressive and prohibitive in ways that cut across the grain of human nature. As a first step to seeing why, consider the family in 'family values'.

The nuclear family is the 'family values' preferred model. Of relatively recent origin – it is a Western urban industrial phenomenon – it is proving notoriously unsuccessful, because it suffers both structural and ethical flaws. The structural flaw is best described by contrast with what it replaces. For much of history the typical family was (and elsewhere in the world still is) a small community, often consisting of more than two generations of people not always related to each other genetically or by marriage, in which the caretaking of children was effected chiefly by other children, grandparents, servants, or economically unproductive (because, say, disabled) members of the household. In such families not all was good or desirable, and often was far the reverse; incest and child sexual abuse, for example, were by no means uncommon (if a man's wife were pregnant or menstruating he might turn to his eldest daughter). In general the facts of life were close to lived experience, sometimes harshly so; disease, mortality and poverty were familiars for most families in most of history. The frequency and pervasiveness of death, especially, gave family life a character quite different from how it now is in the West; for one thing, it made most childhoods and marriages short.

But if there was one thing that extended families were and are good at, it is the dispersal of the kind of stresses that the post-industrial-age minimalist unit suffers from. In the 'family values'; nuclear family, psychological and physical burdens are borne by a small inwardly focused group. Traditional extended families were diffuse in structure, offering varieties of channels for managing emotions and resolving conflicts; but the nuclear family intensifies both by diverting them all inwards.

To this structural flaw is added an ethical flaw relating to the principles that govern the relationships in this enclosed small group. This is that these relationships are intended to be both permanent and exclusive. Divorce and adultery (not to say the even more problematic ways of relieving the claustrophobia – and hence tensions – of nuclear family life, such as drunkenness, violence, and incest) are for good reasons strongly disapproved of, so not only is the group cooped up together in a small emotional space, but the exits and safety valves for the resulting pressures are blocked. The results are familiar enough: 'family breakdown' is a lamented commonplace, on which many social ills are blamed. It is a tribute to the human capacity for deceit and self-denial that complete breakdown occurs in 'only' one out of two nuclear families, although one does not know what greater costs are sometimes paid in keeping the remaining nuclear families together.

In an effort to shore up this inherently unstable family model, the conservative ethic has to stigmatise much that is neutral or even good across the whole range of interpersonal relations and private recreations, not least among them sexuality. The chief aim is to contain the pressures that threaten to explode the nuclear family, if possible by persuading people not to feel them in the first place, but in any case forbidding their expression. A nuclear family works where one of the marital partners is submissive or compromising, and the children are dutiful – and, say, a religious commitment has imposed strong internal controls on temptations that might disrupt these attitudes and the bonds they sustain. A family nourished on religious doctrines which encourage such an outlook is exactly the 'family values' ideal. But it is immediately obvious that it is premised on self-denials and beliefs for which there are no independently good reasons; the only reason for their acceptance is to protect the 'family values' family from breaking down. Urging them, therefore, is rather like urging someone to give up breathing on the grounds that he or she will never thereafter catch 'flu.

Because the modern nuclear family figures so importantly in their outlook, moral conservatives are hostile to divorce, which represents the termination – in their view the failure – of a nuclear-family project. Yet divorce is often a good thing; it gives people a chance to start again, or – which is as great a good, if people could only recognise it as such – to live alone; solitary life is not necessarily lonely life, but can be a strong and productive mode of existence, and very peaceful.

Divorce allows freedom and flexibility for everyone, but especially for women, to make changes when change is needed in their domestic arrangements. Marriage without the possibility of divorce is a life-sentence based on decisions made (usually) at a time when the participants' judgement was immature, and also influenced by pheromones or fashions. Without divorce, the result is unchangeable, no matter what new circumstances arise. Divorce is often a miserable experience because it signals the loss of affections important to one or both parties; but it is even more wretched when society makes divorce difficult, so adding to the problems of those experiencing it.

Like abortion, divorce is a question of personal freedom. It is about people starting afresh, remedying mistakes, getting back on course with other decisions and choices, to construct lives worth living.

There is no better or more eloquent case for divorce than the one made by the poet John Milton. In 1643 he made a visit to the country home of one Richard Powell, who owed him the then very large sum of £500. He came away without his money, but with Powell's seventeen-year-old daughter

Mary as his wife. (He was aged thirty-five.) A month later Mary returned to her father's house, and the marriage was at an end. She had been a child in a large bustling household; he had been expecting to be ministered to as he pursued his work in long hours of studious silence. Moreover Milton found that he had mistaken the potential of Mary's mind, which he had hoped would grow to be a companion to his in intellectual and literary interests. A year later Milton published a tract arguing the legitimacy of divorce on grounds other than adultery, then the only permissible ground. He took as his text on the true nature of marriage neither the one favoured by Catholics, 'Be fruitful and multiply,' nor the one favoured by Lutherans, 'Better to marry than to burn,' but the far earlier 'It is not good for man to be alone.' And on this basis he argued,

> In God's intention a meet and happy conversation is the chief and noblest end of marriage ... The chief society thereof is in the soul rather than in the body, and the greatest breach thereof is unfitness of mind rather than defect of body ... we know it is not the joining of another body will remove loneliness, but the uniting of another compliable mind; and that it is not a blessing but a torment, nay a base and brutish condition to be one flesh, unless where nature can in some measure fix and unite the disposition ... What a violent and cruel thing it is to force the continuing of those together whom God and nature in the gentlest end of marriage never joined.

Well, this argument has long since been won, but it is surprising how very recent it is that the recognition of the deep underlying truth in what Milton said has been translated into concrete terms. And yet there remain those who wish to make divorce more difficult on the ground that it might help some couples stay together who are 'merely going through a bad patch'. One has to remember that one way out of bad patches is the defeat of some part of one of the couple, the submission to a compromise, and the loss of a hope, which in the best scheme of things we would not wish to countenance.

There would be no divorce if there were no marriage. Marriage is a central pillar of the 'family values' view, not merely in the desirable sense of a long-term committed relationship, but as a legally constituted one that controls the age and sex of the parties to it (it says who can enter it, and when) and dictates what they can and must do in it, and on what terms, if any, they can leave it. So viewed, legal marriage looks like a monstrous public interference in personal relations, and it is surprising how many people still go in for it. Aside from their religious interests (and – more trivially – the fun of dressing up for the ceremony, the usefulness of getting presents, or the unmeaning claim that 'getting married shows commitment'), couples when asked why, instead of just living together, they choose legal marriage, tend to cite the interests of children they might have. Bastardy considerations might once have made sense of this point, but are an irrelevance now.

The truth, no doubt, is that people continue to marry merely because it is traditional and in so doing they perpetuate an institution which originated for inequitable social and economic reasons, chief among them to control the sexual activity and fertility of women, and thus to ensure that the property men bequeath has a better chance of going to children who are truly theirs. If there were a clearer sense of the history of the institution, the reasons people have for entering into the legal version of marriage (marriage as a tripartite contract between two persons and the state, giving

the latter rights over the couple's relationship and goods)
would seem less persuasive.

In the early Christian Church people got married by
declaring their intention to live together. By medieval times
people with property made a major public show of marriage
for dynastic and inheritance purposes; this is where the
chastity of wives mattered too, to ensure that the property-
owner was passing what he owned to heirs of his own flesh.
The property-less had many different ways of partnering
each other, with or without the benefit of Church or state
sanction. But as wealth generalised, so the need for uniform-
ity in such arrangements became more pressing; and it was
in the mid-eighteenth century that at last a law was passed
in England requiring all persons to marry according to a
common formula giving the state its rights in the matter.

All this follows from a sense of the term 'marriage' that is
rather reductive, applying as it does to the institutional and
legal aspects of the case. In a richer and fuller sense, marriage
is the coming together of people who wish to be together and
to share life's projects, to pool resources, to help and enjoy
each other, and to raise children together, irrespective of
whether or not they have signed pieces of paper or been given
the sanction of the municipal authorities. To some these
latter amenities are more insults than otherwise, interfering
as they do with the voluntary and affectional nature of the
choice they make, every day refreshed and reasserted, to be
in that intimate union with the chosen other. Marriage is
more truly and pointfully this latter free association than it
is the anachronistic matter of state – and Church – having
fingers in the pie, regulating and dictating its terms.

Mention of the Church pointedly reminds one that in any
case the idea of coercive regulation of sexuality and fertility is an ancient obsession of the religions, dating from the
unhappy accident that the first of the three Religions of the

Book (Judaism, Christianity and Islam) was primitively a herding and flock-keeping community, for whom the fertility of the livestock mattered hugely. That is why Onan was struck dead for spilling his seed on the ground instead of directing it to the fertilising of his dead brother's wife; and it is why the Roman Catholic Church has regarded masturbation as a crime worse than rape, because the latter can at least issue in pregnancy. From such distortions of value come the distorting institutions aimed at governing even our intimacies.

There is one thing that women, especially, are inclined to say in favour of the institutional sense of the term 'marriage', and that is that it provides a measure of protection against the consequences of relationship breakdown if they are in the vulnerable situation of having young children and no or little income of their own. Then the state can give the matrimonial home and a part of the ex-spouse's income to the woman, in the interests of her children before all else. This is a strong point; but one would have thought that independently of the institution of marriage there is a question of natural justice in the case that would be enforceable by civil remedy. If either parent abandons a relationship in which there are young children, he or she should be expected to contribute in a properly effective way to their care. This is indisputable. It is also all that can be expected; thus, if a woman leaves her husband, and he has to care for two small children, she should certainly play her part in the financing of their upbringing at very least, until they have attained adulthood. Whether she should be expected to subsidise her former husband thereafter is an entirely different question.

But questions about children's interests always touch a chord, and are therefore important to 'family values' supporters, not only in their defence of nuclear-family marriage but in their correlative attack on one-parent families. Children's interests, they claim, are served best by the former and are at risk in the latter.

Children's interests are certainly of very great importance indeed. But is it true that they are best served *only* by the 'family values' conception of their welfare? What matters to children is being loved and cared for, so that they are provided with stability, support, confidence, sensible social-isation, a good diet, and opportunities to play and learn. It does not matter how many parents they have or even whether the person or people who look after them are their biological parents, so long as the relationship is a secure and enduring one. Biological parturition is no guarantee of the social skills required for parenting.

The problem with one-parent families is the absence not of another parent, but of resources – in short, poverty. Social hostility – with its roots in religious condemnation – to sex and childbirth outside marriage leaves a stigma, at very least as representing a social problem and a burden on the community, to say nothing of supposed difficulties that the children of one-parent families will cause in future. The result is economic punishment; moral conservatives are reluctant to 'subsidise the irresponsibility' of unmarried women and teenage girls who get pregnant, even more so when they do it more than once. This reluctance amounts, one is obliged to say, to a Canute-like opposition to biological forces. It is in animal nature to mate, and hence sometimes to repro-duce; only human animals try to control sexual activity and reproduction for social, religious, or moral reasons; and only humans punish deviation from what they have decided, in some place at some point in history, to regard as a norm.

There could be few better investments in society than pro-viding the kind of help to all families who need it, whatever their composition, that would lift them clear of the threat posed by poverty. Poverty produces stress, conflicts, inter-personal ruptures, dependence on forms of escapism that reaches as far as drug use, crime (a great deal of it related to the need for resources to secure those escapes), and all the attendant limitations on life that being imprisoned by these things generates. The contrast with a life that is provided with more than the essentials is marked; for in the latter case children and adults alike have the kind of psychological space and assurance to look around them, and see that the world is a bigger and more opportunity-providing place than are any local geographies of limitation.

Social anxieties about one-parent families are also anxieties about 'sink estates', problem schools, youth crime, drugs, teenage sex, and whatever else contributes to that familiar constellation. Conservative moralists use their ideal of the family to promote and justify their views about these matters. On each of these questions the 'family values' view is as disputable as its view of the family itself. I consider some of them in turn in the next chapter, beginning with the question of sex and morals.

CHAPTER 7

Sex and Sexuality

If sexual activity were allowed its natural place in human life it would consume considerably less time and energy than it now does. Sex occupies an absurdly inflated part of the moral horizon, and in many respects is surrounded by muddle and even misery, because prohibitions, anxieties, and what amounts to social rationing exaggerate its importance ('the hungry individual thinks only of food'), and in some cases distort it – for frustrated instincts are more prone to seek unusual, sometimes harmful, outlets than more easily satisfiable ones.

The kindness of nature has made sexual activity pleasurable, not just to encourage reproduction but to promote bonding and, plausibly, health also. Our closest primate relatives, bonobo chimpanzees, enjoy frequent sexual encounters as a means of bonding and recreation, just as with humans. Among other primates mating activity is governed by the oestrus cycle, which renders female sexual interest periodic. Otherwise chimpanzees, gorillas, and orang-utans do not moralise, still less agonise, about sex, but simply get on with it when hormones prompt.

Matters are greatly more complex with humans, of course, and there is no clear answer to the question: what is the 'natural place' of sex in human life? A woman's potential investment in sexual activity, with its possible sequels of pregnancy and childcare, is so heavy that it seems natural to expect her to be more circumspect than a man about engaging in sex – at the very least, when contraception is unavailable or unreliable. If some characteristic kinds of male homosexual activity are any guide to male sexuality in general, men are rather like bonobos in being apt to engage in frequent casual sexual encounters, with little emotional commitment. On this view, the argument might be that heterosexual males differ from their homosexual brothers only in having, as a rule, less opportunity for sex, owing to conventions and the restraints imposed by potential partners.

Studies suggest that, if women's potential investment in sex is reduced by effective contraception and greater economic independence, their behaviour changes. In particular, wherever women attain equal status in business and the professions, their sexual behaviour comes increasingly to resemble that of men – participation in casual sexual encounters, short affairs, more than one affair at a time, and sometimes even in such respects as employing prostitutes while on business trips (often female prostitutes, it seems). The similarities do not end there; it also appears that increasingly many women business executives suffer stress-induced male-pattern hair loss.

There is interesting evidence from a different quarter: that a surprising percentage of children are fathered by someone other than their mother's husband or resident partner. The exact percentage is difficult to know, because published figures range from 12 per cent to as much as 30 per cent in two studies published in the early 1990s; the latter figure strikes one as implausibly high. But parallel studies show the same pattern among birds. And reflection suggests that it obviously makes good genetic sense; if humans follow the patterns discernible elsewhere in the animal kingdom, it appears that nature remains stronger among them than convention.

These points suggest that men and women differ in sexual behaviour only when the latter are obliged to consider consequences. The advance of science has made these factors contingent, not essential; anatomy is no longer destiny. So everything one wishes to say about sexual morality applies equally to both sexes.

Sexual activity is not morally neutral in itself; it is – when consensual – a good, because it can be pleasurable and establishes bonds between people. But in some societies, chiefly Judaeo-Christian ones, it is complicated by the influence of ancient beliefs and practices. People are more interested in sex than informed about it, and, while ignorance remains, its urgencies and ecstasies make it equally tempting and threatening. Sexual pleasure, said Aristotle, subverts rationality, and his remark is the premise for persistent anxiety in certain outlooks: if sex is irrational it is a threat to order and therefore authority. In consequence sexuality has been constrained by laws and customs in many cultures throughout history, with Christianity among the worst offenders. In AD 1800 more people were hanged in England for sodomy than for murder; in the Middle East adulterers can still be stoned to death; in most countries censorship of art continues on 'obscenity' grounds. As a further consequence, sex is shrouded in hypocrisy, guilt, exploitation, anxiety, and perversion, adding fuel to its fires and making it a real rather than merely a perceived problem.

Despite the increased openness that has permitted objective research into human sexuality, there is still no widely accepted theory about it upon which personal decision- or public policy-making can rely. Yet there has never existed greater need for such a theory, because sex-related dilemmas currently offer Western society dramatic challenges: Aids, venereal diseases, abortion, contraception, surrogate motherhood, artificial fertilisation, homosexual demands for the right to marry and adopt children, teenage sex and pregnancy, sexual harassment, marital and 'date' rape, child abuse, pornography – the list of concerns is long, and even so omits the fact that 'ordinary' sexual relations are themselves still subject to repressive and muddled thinking.

One attempt to understand the place of sex in social life applies to it the theory of rational choice, where 'rational' means the appropriate fitting, conscious or otherwise, of means to ends. It may seem quixotic to apply such a theory to sex, given assumptions about the latter's irrationality, but although sexual instincts are indeed at least non-rational, the strategies people adopt to satisfy them are otherwise. Consider the analogy of hunger: we do not will hunger, but we take thought about appeasing it.

Such theorists offer analyses in cost-benefit terms. Among the benefits of sex are pleasure and progeny; among the costs, the effort of finding a mate, defeating rivals, and tending offspring. A simple example is afforded by 'opportunistic homosexuality' among prisoners who, usually heterosexual, behave homosexually because in the circumstances benefits outweigh cost. So stated, the theory seems simplistic, but studies employing the model are surprisingly powerful in explaining differences in, for example, styles of marriage and prostitution in different societies. One unsurprising conclusion is that the status of women is a principal determinant. In societies where wives are uneducated and much younger than their husbands, companionate marriage does not exist, so sex is formal and occasional. Women are sequestered to 'protect their virtue', but men are freely permitted extramarital sex. In societies where women have high status, as in the contemporary West, companionate marriage is the norm, so that courtesan services are no longer in demand, and prostitution becomes a source of variety or specialist sex, supplementing (even, in some views, protecting) marriage.

Such theories provide useful perspectives, but they have not freed sexual attitudes from ancient taboos and restrictions. Public nudity is a crime; public exposure of genitals by a live human male is regarded with particular concern; as these words are written, public portrayal of an erect male penis is illegal. Elaborate social and legal barriers control how, when, where, and with whom sexual activity is permissible. People are taught to be offended by public displays of sex; a person who might be shocked to see copulation at the roadside will watch it in a film, shielded by the relative unreality of celluloid. These attitudes, as a result not least of religious moral teaching over centuries, are deeply ingrained.

Not all the reasons for seeking to manage sex and sexuality are bad ones. Sex both creates relationships and – but largely because of the taboos and anxieties that surround it – destroys them. In Western societies marriage and marriage-like partnerships are based on mutual attraction; what we call romance is, in prosaic dress, sexual infatuation prompted more by biochemistry than by conscious choice. Sexual infatuation is the hot torch that first welds people together, but passion is temporary, and the interesting question is: what conjunction remains when the alloy has cooled? If infatuation matures into friendship, the basis of the settled domestic affections is to hand. But lovers not infrequently find that, when the blaze of desire dies, only ashes remain; and they sensibly move on.

But what of sex and the domestic affections? As noted above in connection with 'family values', the monogamous principle in Judaeo-Christian societies is an attempt to pre-serve the family, but because of its restrictive view of sex it often achieves the opposite. Monogamy entails 'sexual fidelity', which means restriction of one's sexual expression exclusively to one other person. Historically, women were the main target of this restriction, to ensure (as already noted, but the point is an insistent one for our culture) that their offspring genetically belonged to their husbands; but it is chiefly in Christianity that it applies also to men. Ideals of chastity, continence, celibacy, virginity are as old as Christianity itself, and in their absence something approaching them has, it seems, to be maintained – a partial celibacy, a mimicked continence.

For both men and women these restrictions on sexual expression constitute an unnatural and unkind arrange-ment, especially after initial sexual infatuation quietens and normal interest in the wider world returns. By link-ing sexuality with the domestic emotions and the social institution of monogamous marriage – along with expecta-tions of mutual lifelong romance, which sexual infidelity is believed to destroy – the settled domestic relationships become a trade-off: if you desire to form and preserve such a relationship, you must cramp or deny your normal sexual expression.

This is an absurd, often a destructive, and sometimes a tragic confusion of two quite different matters. In practice this Judaeo-Christian attempt to restrict sex is largely unsuccessful. Most parties to marriage-like relationships have affairs, commit adultery, visit prostitutes, or some-how circumvent the restriction, having to be deceitful and hypocritical in the process – thereby risking damage to their domestic relationships, which is what few of them desire. So in a 'family values' dispensation the choices for com-bining nature's kindly gift of sex with the great pleasures and benefits of domestic relationships are: (a) marriage breakdown; (b) deceit and hypocrisy; or (c) an unnatural self-denial.

The principal solutions are so-called 'open marriage', or a second partner (a lover). It is claimed that the former does not work; we certainly hear of the failures, but the successes only become apparent when we read biographies. In the monogamous Western tradition, where sexual attitudes are so ingrained that few can think differently, such arrangements are little tolerated. Accordingly, one has to suppose that the best alternative to hypocrisy is discretion and good manners – of the kind that civilised couples have always practised anyway.

But obviously it would be best if, first, it were recognised that domestic relations do not essentially depend on (keeping up the pretence of) sexual fidelity, and second, if society was rescued from the view that one person is entitled to exclusive ownership of another's sexual expression. The painful choice – the tragic conflict – that this view forces is an evil. The desideratum is to live in a dispensation of things where the settled domestic affections are not inconsistent with normal human sexuality.

None of this denies the importance of fidelity in domestic relationships, in the sense of commitment to a partnership of shared life and goals, and of deep mutual private loyalties. Much of the value in domestic affection rests on the security thus provided. But fidelity in this sense is not the same thing as exclusive ownership of another's sexual expression. This essential point is, at great cost, almost universally overlooked.

In most other cultures in the world the problem is solved – except in very few cases, for men only – by polygamy, concubinage, or the social acceptability of extramarital sex. If saner attitudes were to prevail in the West, they would have to be applied equitably between the sexes; the removal of anatomy from destiny, as remarked above, makes this possible. And as implied by the opening remarks, taking the pressure off sex would undoubtedly make it look less large in general. Moral conservatives of course think the opposite; they think they would be stepping over writhing couples in every street, which is why they keep the motors of our present unsatisfactory dispensation running.

Two of the largest margins of sexual life, homosexuality and prostitution, have always been targets for moral conservatives, who for millennia have succeeded in turning the weight not just of custom but of law against both. In the Judaeo-Christian tradition prostitutes were sometimes stoned to death. No single method for killing homosexuals regularly established itself, although hanging later became usual. It is a profound anomaly that classical Greece, a civilisation admired by the West and claimed as its cultural ancestor, permitted – indeed, encouraged – not merely homosexuality but pederasty. There are contemporary non-Western cultures where similar views remain; in one Papuan society, for example, it is the practice for men to 'supply seed' to boys entrusted to their tutelage, so that they can father children in their turn. This is a literal version of what the Greeks saw in more educational terms (although the relationship between men and boys in Greece was usually physical too).

These are customs that many will think well superseded, and for good reasons. Social life and the nature of its structural relationships, including the prolongation of childhood into relatively late adolescence because of the complexity of the education required for membership of modern society, adds to our moral rejection of these options a deep pragmatic one also.

It is a pity history is so selective, though; for just one

example of something vile which, nevertheless, contemporary moral conservatives tolerate with equanimity – some, indeed, regularly practise it – consider the genital mutilation of millions of boys and girls, which flourishes today in religious practices of circumcision.

The case against homosexuality is that it is 'unnatural'. The argument is simple: male and female sex organs are mutually adapted anatomically for the purpose of reproduction. Since the organs of two men or two women are not thus adapted, and cannot result in reproduction, congress of any kind between them is 'unnatural'. The same reasoning prohibits heterosexual practices that do not have reproduction as a possible outcome.

If this argument were generalised, it would be disgusting – and, by parity of reasoning, ought therefore to be illegal – to ride a bicycle or blow a whistle, since these activities are not what legs or lips are biologically 'for'.

But the best analogy is eating. We eat to nourish our bodies; but also to enjoy tastes and textures, to relax, to meet friends, to converse. One needs just so many calories and vitamins each day, but one also enjoys sampling Indian and Chinese and Italian cuisines. One may discover a taste for Chinese, and a distaste for Indian, food. So it is with sex. It is natural to enjoy sexual pleasure, as it is to enjoy food; and the purpose of sex, as with eating, is not exclusively the minimum that either is 'for'.

These points show that appeals to 'nature' provide no ground for hostility to homosexuality. The real source of hostility is religious and social, and, as we have seen, only *some* religions and societies are hostile. In them the result is, or has frequently been, persecution of individuals on the mere ground of their difference from the majority in regard to taste or choice.

Hostility to homosexuality has a number of sources, but

one of them is that it threatens the model of interpersonal relations at the core of the 'family values' ethos. Hostility to prostitution (chiefly in the realms of anglophone Protestant Christianity) has the same roots. Yet the irony is that prostitution, at least in part, flourishes precisely because of 'family values' – as suggested above, by providing one way of releasing the pressures caused by nuclear-family life under a restrictive sexual morality.

In some American states, and in Britain, prostitution remains legally circumscribed, the legal sanctions expressing the opposition and disgust of moral conservatives. As a result it is riper for the hands of organised crime. Except for its financial aspects, the casual, uncommitted nature of interaction between prostitutes and their clients mirrors the cottaging experience of homosexual men, which, as noted, perhaps says something about the nature of male sexuality in general. This appears to be recognised by society, which implicitly accepts what is sometimes described as the 'hygienic' function of prostitution; but it does so in secret and in shame, which means that the question is not sensibly addressed, but fudged. It is obvious on the least reflection that prostitution should be legal, not only to enhance the health and safety of both practitioners and clients, but also to end the waste of police time and the burden on the legal system. All the reasons that moral conservatives have for wishing to control prostitution legally – the supposed threat to family life, the supposed threat to minors, and the fact that girls might be forced into sex work by economic conditions or exploitative pimps – will remain whether or not prostitution is legal, with the one difference that the third of these will always be much worse if it is illegal.

It must be supposed that some of those who work in the sex industry do so by choice. They provide a service that will always be in demand, and, because they might wish to work together with colleagues in safe and comfortable surroundings, it seems only sensible to allow brothels. In societies where prostitution is legal there has been no social collapse of the kind moral conservatives fear. States with restrictive laws might take that fact alone as a reason to reconsider.

The same considerations apply to pornography, defined as 'sexually explicit material designed to cause sexual arousal'. In countries with liberal laws on pornography there has been no social implosion, nor has there been as a result of the wide availability of pornography on the internet, where it is the largest single type of content. So one main argument against it collapses. There are other and better arguments against it: that it conveys abusive images of women, and involves exploitation of the people who produce it. These points are important, for abuse and exploitation are evils. But they are evils because they are abuse and exploitation, not because they involve sex. If there were sexually explicit material made by happy people who grew rich providing a service to contented clients, it would on this reasoning be unexceptionable. If pornography were legal, the likelihood of its being produced in an exploitative way diminishes.

Some feminists, in unaccustomed alliance with conservatives and the Churches, oppose liberalisation of pornography on the ground not just that it involves a denigrating portrayal of women, but that this promotes rape and violence against them. Here again what is objectionable is the denigration and the violence, rather than the sexual content of either. One can make a case against any group being portrayed in any such way; and one can and should resolutely combat incitements to harm. At the same time, it has to be possible that there should be sexually explicit material that does not incite to hatred or violence. The facts again speak for themselves: in countries where restrictions on pornography have been lifted – for example, Denmark – violent sexual crime has diminished.

It goes without saying that the exploitation of children for pornographic purposes is a moral evil of the worst kind, and is totally unacceptable. Condign action against it is justified by the dimensions of abuse and harm that are not to be tolerated in connection with the interests of children. Adults non-exploitatively and non-harmfully viewing or engaging in the explicit portrayal of sexual activities is an entirely different matter, and the two should be kept separate.

There is a struggle within feminism itself over the nature and legitimacy of attitudes to pornography and, by association, to female heterosexuality in general. A premise of one strand in radical feminism has been that heterosexuality is a vehicle of male exploitation and is therefore intrinsically wrong, like a modern version of original sin. To be properly free, this argument goes, women must liberate themselves from heterosexuality. In urging their sisters to deny access to their bodies – allegedly regarded by men as mere receptacles for their secretions and desires – such feminists urge their sisters to think of their own bodies as dustbins and betrayers: dustbins, because of what men variously wish to deposit in them; and betrayers, because women's bodies desire those deposits.

But it would not be too great a temerity for a male author to speculate that most women who want what feminists rightly want for womankind – justice, equality, respect – also wish to enjoy their heterosexuality without guilt. One way to do so is to accept the nature, and assert the value, of female heterosexuality as part of repudiating ill-based, harmful, outdated attitudes to human sexuality in general. One source of the oppressive nature of relations between the sexes is the traditional morality of a social arrangement that feminist thinkers have correctly identified as 'patri-archal' – that is, as serving the interests of a male-oriented perspective on relations between the sexes, justified and defended by conservative morality. It is remarkable how persistent patriarchal attitudes are, for they remain both in the minutiae of life, not least domestic life, in the great majority of societies, and in its large structures; even in the developed West women constantly find themselves suffering a variety of discriminations stemming from patriarchy (and this, among other things, despite doing better in education than male counterparts).

Everything so far amounts to saying that sex is an amenity of life that we handle badly and should allow to go free, whereupon we will soon find it less of a preoccupation. But the subject cannot be left without registering the point, obvious but important, that sex is only a good when it is consensual.

The worst examples of non-consensual sex are rape and what might be called constructive rape, which occurs when the consent given is not properly informed or free. Into this second category fall many cases of child abuse, because it cannot be plausible to think that children – depending on age or level of understanding – are in as good a position as normally placed older people to reflect on the choices in-volved. This degree of paternalism is justified by the fact that, even if some children are in fact so placed, it is better to start with the reverse assumption as a way of protecting their interests prospectively.

Rape and sexual abuse are peculiarly horrible because they violate physical and psychological privacy, make the victim the object of a particularly loathsome attitude on the part of the perpetrator, by which he (usually he) treats the victim in the most reductively instrumental way, without a jot of thought for the significance of the harm he does. And in the case of children there is also a deep breach of trust. If the one great sin is harm to others, these crimes are close to murder.

Consensual adult sexual behaviour is a very different matter. It is painfully obvious that legal and social strictures upon it need reform. Given the way that the law has been called in aid by moral conservatives over the centuries to limit or prohibit human sexuality, or steer its expression in the direction of their own tastes and prejudices, reform is especially needed in all those jurisdictions still influenced by their legacy. These are chiefly the anglophone Western jurisdictions.

Consider the fact that sodomy between consenting males over the age of twenty-one is legal in Britain, but between men and women is punishable by life imprisonment. (Matters are still worse for offenders in the US state of Georgia; they can be executed.) This is not the only anomaly in the law relating to sexual matters, but since it is in effect a dead letter it is far from the most serious. The age of consent for homosexuals, their rights to marry one another and to adopt children, are far more pressing questions; and so is the confusion over marital and date rape, pornography, obscenity, and prostitution. In each of these areas reform is required to liberate attitudes as much as practices, and to alleviate the tensions that make them problematic.

One of the barriers to reform is the existence of the tabloid press. Its rabid attitudes and the hypocritical way it titillates readers about what it pretends to condemn – 'Vicar in sex romp with choirboys' – mean that politicians, not a notably courageous race, are reluctant to institute reform, having no wish to prompt such headlines as 'Government opens floodgates to vice'. The tabloid press subverts discussion of important public questions, a fact we have had to learn to live with; but on the question of bringing sanity and humanity into the law there can be no temporising.

The tabloid formula of salaciousness masquerading as moral outrage is not, however, the main barrier to reform. The main barrier is that queer beast 'public opinion', which the media half follow and half form. 'Public opinion' on any given matter is in reality the opinion of a decided and emphatic minority, whose claim to the moral high ground on the matter in question, usually staked in the name of religion and organised into effective lobbies – as in the United States – makes it formidable. Moral conservatives succeed in giving enough of the rest of us an uneasy feeling that *perhaps* such and such is wrong; and a seed of doubt is sufficient for inaction, because few are courageous in matters they have not much pondered, and it always seems easier to follow what appears to be majority opinion than to be isolated. For this reasons, liberal reform has to be not just generous but bold, as the next example – that of drugs – especially shows.

CHAPTER 8

Drugs

The question of drugs is an appropriate one to comment on as a target of opprobrium for moral conservatives, because it affords a good illustration of the way conservatism creates rather than solves problems. Actually, neither the use nor the abuse of drugs, legal or otherwise, is a *moral* problem; it is, rather, a practical one – although in a quite different way one might regard the *abuse* of drugs as an *ethical* problem.

By 'drugs' I mean opium and its derivatives, cocaine and such substances as LSD, 'Ecstasy', amphetamines, solvents, tranquillisers and anything else people use to alter their states of mind and mood, whether they become addicted to them or not; and so the list includes alcohol, nicotine and caffeine. Drugs fall into three classes depending upon whether they are narcotic, stimulant or hallucinogenic in effect. There are many other substances in what we eat and drink that have such effects, but they are generally much milder.

The distinction drawn between substances now controlled by law and those that are not is the result not of principle but of history, and is otherwise arbitrary. Alcohol and nicotine are arguably more dangerous to health than marijuana, and the latter has been found to have medicinal value – as have the opium derivatives and cocaine for analgesia and anaesthesia. So the reason that alcohol and nicotine are legal (for adults) while the latter are not is simply that they have been used more widely and for longer in Western societies, and efforts to ban them have proved unacceptable to the populace. The distinction is therefore not a well-based one, so already the rationality of public policy on drug use and misuse is questionable.

Drugs first came under legal control in Britain in 1868, not to regulate their use but to protect the professional status of pharmacists, who desired the sole right to dispense them. Opium was widely used in the form of laudanum, and heroin was developed from opium towards the end of the century. During the First World War soldiers in the trenches of Flanders and Picardy tempered the horrors they faced by using opiates and – as did Freud in fact and Sherlock Holmes in fiction – cocaine. This prompted a Defence of the Realm Act banning the public sale of these drugs for the first time. Anti-drug legislation thus began as a means of ensuring that young men would be fit to murder one another. For several decades prior to 1914 moral conservatives had been campaigning in Britain and America for prohibition – principally of alcohol, but there also existed a British society for the suppression of cocaine. The war gave them their chance; their time had at last come. In the United States the great folly of Prohibition was enacted soon after the war, and in the same mood laws began to be passed in most Western countries against opiates, cocaine and marijuana.

Since then many substances have joined the list. When these laws were first enacted in the 1920s the incidence of drugs use and abuse was relatively small, and in the case of addiction was regarded rather as a medical than a legal problem. One result of the prohibition of drugs has been more rapid growth in their use, by the familiar mechanisms of marketing by criminal organisations, and the attractiveness of the forbidden.

The disaster of Prohibition in America should have taught the world lessons enough on this score. Not only does prohibition lay the foundations of a massive criminal industry, but it turns millions of ordinary people into lawbreakers also, and imposes high costs in money and human life.

In the case of alcohol prohibition these developments were rapid; when Prohibition was lifted, the criminal gangs it created turned to other activities, including drug-running. Here development was slower, but as sure. The business practice of creating and fostering a market for commodities is adopted by illegitimate just as by legitimate businesses. Selling all kinds of drugs – alcohol and cigarettes as well as cocaine and marijuana – includes focus on the young, making their use fashionable and desirable. All these substances provide relief from the pressures and complexities of life, and induce states that are intrinsically pleasant. Add a garnish of social disapproval, and their attractions are complete.

The criminalisation of drugs thus creates an enormous problem where a far lesser one previously existed. By providing opportunities for organised crime, and turning many users into criminals – principally those who become addicted and who therefore have to work hard at mugging or theft to pay for their habit – it entangles the police, courts and customs authorities in mighty and expensive labours.

All these problems would be abolished at a stroke by decriminalisation. What would follow? Would the entire populace suddenly become addicted to heroin? Of course not. Most people who wish to take drugs already do so; most people who regularly consume currently legal drugs – alcohol, nicotine, caffeine – do so sensibly, and manage to lead normal lives despite their addictions and the health problems that follow. Just as one encourages people not to smoke or drink excessively, so one would encourage people not to take heroin or cocaine; and just as one prosecutes people for driving a motor car or causing a public nuisance under the influence of alcohol, so one would prosecute those who misbehaved under the influence of cocaine or LSD.

A true story illustrates one of many aspects to this debate. The sixteen-year-old son of a friend of mine decided that he wished to try heroin. He and a friend bought some, took it home, and administered it to themselves. Unfamiliarity with the substance meant that they did not know how much to take, and they were not aware that they had purchased a particularly pure form. The result was a massive overdose, and both died.

If the heroin had come from a pharmacy in a packet containing a standard purity, with instructions on the side concerning the safe amount to be taken, they would not have died. As it is, they did; and a criminal had walked off with their money.

There is another thought. Colombia, Afghanistan and other countries produce and sell the ingredients for the drugs illegally taken all over the world. Efforts to suppress the drug trade – a doomed and costly battle – involve trying to destroy crops at source. Imagine the effect on farmers in these poor countries following decriminalisation; and imagine too how the criminal and terrorist organisations which depend on revenue from illegal drug production and trade would be affected.

I suggested that drug *ab*use is not a moral problem, but an ethical one. By this I mean that people who depend upon (rather than occasionally employ for recreational purposes) exogenous chemical means to attain well-being or fulfil-ment, or to escape from difficulties, are in a sad case, either because they genuinely need the support of the community in some respect, or because they lack the intelligence or courage to attain life's satisfactions under their own steam. Dependence on readily ingestible sources of life's amenities, at least in any regular way, strikes me as either pitiable or contemptible. But neither is a reason for making it illegal.

Forbidding people to eat or drink what they wish, or to seek certain pleasures, is a gross form of interference. One must suggest limits, exactly as one does with alcohol: on the age at which people might be supposed capable of informed choices, and on the acceptable degree of the public consequences of making those choices, under the ever-present condition that what anyone does must not interfere with or harm others. But, although there can be justification for regulating matters in these minimal ways, there can be none for forbidding them.

This discussion illustrates two points. The first is that prohibition is a creator of problems, not their solution. This insight applies almost universally. To lift prohibitions is not to deregulate entirely; any group of people who discussed their joint and several interests reasonably among themselves would conclude that certain minimum rules are required. But the presumption has to be on the side of permission, not prohibition; every limitation has to be exceedingly well justified.

The second point expands the ethical remark already made. It is that we may not wish, and in the clearest picture of ourselves ought not to wish, to be people fundamentally dependent on quick outside fixes for our reliefs and satisfactions. This is a point about autonomy: if you are a heroin addict, your well-being is at the mercy of a powder; you are in a heteronymous state, governed by something external. The good life for an individual must include self-government to the maximum degree consistent with its community setting. A life of dependency on drugs, whether alcohol or heroin, is not such a life, and seems a peculiarly feeble and contemptible way to live.

CHAPTER 9

Death and Dying

The problems so far discussed are problems about life and living. Problems about death and dying seem even more vexed, not least because they are more influenced by religious attitudes. The lack of clarity in discussion of the ethics of death reflects the subjects' emotional significance; it is no surprise that the liberal–conservative disagreement here is especially sharp.

Although there are some accidents and diseases that kill people quickly, and although the mechanisms of senescence can bring gentle endings to life, it is also and often enough the case that dying is protracted, difficult and painful, sometimes involving unendurable physical and psychological distress. In such cases it is not only the victim who suffers, but the loving witnesses.

Contrast the case in which a person has elected to die before some paralysing disease has made speech or swallowing impossible, or before age has leached away the mind so that the surviving shell trembles and drools, perhaps fractionally aware of its indignities. In this case the subject is able to say farewell, to share the parting, and to go with the painless ease that medical science can so simply provide. It is a devoutly wishable consummation.

Here is an example of such a case. A woman in her seventies, agonisingly crippled but alert despite reliance on drugs, considered her predicament, balanced it with the pleasures that life still afforded – and chose to die before these last were gone too. After discussion, her family and closest friends accepted her decision. In the week before the chosen day they came to see her, and wrote affectionate letters; on the day itself there was a gathering, with reminiscences and poetry, and farewells. Then she was left with friends who had agreed to sit with her when she took her last dose of barbiturates. As she slipped into unconsciousness they read aloud and held her hands; within an hour she stopped breathing.

This is a case of assisted suicide, which is the best form of euthanasia in that it has the conscious elective participation of the subject. Involuntary euthanasia occurs when someone is unable to express the desire to die, but is in such a terrible state that a quick means of ending life is administered. There are many cases where both forms of euthanasia are completely justified. In jurisdictions where, nevertheless, euthanasia is illegal (even if widely practised; which is almost everywhere – for human pity is stronger than law), many people are needlessly condemned to suffering by the chief anti-euthanasia argument: that legalised euthanasia might be abused.

And so indeed it might. Is that a reason for letting unrelievable suffering continue or increase? Or is it a reason for so arranging matters that abuse (everything, legal or otherwise, is open to at least some abuse: humans are endlessly ingenious) is minimised?

Opponents of euthanasia imagine that inconveniently ageing parents will be destroyed like unwanted kittens; that hard-pressed hospitals will routinely increase morphine dosages not just in clearly terminal cases but in long-drawn-out, doubtful, expensive ones too; that the ill, in a temporary fit of gloom, will make a mistakenly permanent decision; that someone will ask for a last injection just weeks before a medical breakthrough. These anxieties increase the sum of human agony throughout the tender-minded West. Less forgivable than these anxieties is the superstitious belief that there is a deity who, having given life, is alone authorised to take it away, and if it wishes anyone's life to end in indignity and suffering, so be it.

In poor countries, where there is not the technology to prolong life, the dilemma arises less often. What makes the euthanasia debate more acute is precisely the fact that we are technically able both to kill and to keep alive with relative facility. It is the endless medical dilemma: should we do or not do what we can do? Does 'can' ever mean 'must', and if so, when?

The rule here should be that, when we are satisfied that euthanasia is the right, merciful, humane course, we should do it. It is not beyond human wit to devise thoughtful controls. There will be difficult cases; there could be mistakes; abuse might occur. But that is par for the course in human affairs. The belief that it is mere quantity of life that matters blinds us to the recognition that we can and must accept defeasibility in the euthanasia case as we do everywhere else. One act of genuine mercy, in which we help a person escape agony or indignity or both, will justify us.

Because of the significance of this question it is worth repeating what is centrally at issue in it. Euthanasia literally means 'a good death', and in that sense everyone hopes for euthanasia in the end, usually by preference a naturally occurring easy and painless death after a healthy old age. A suicide or assisted suicide might go wrong, if not properly carried out, and result in suffering for the subject – and thus not count as euthanasia in the literal sense.

Euthanasia has come mainly to mean deliberate acts or omissions that result in someone's death, as when an elderly patient with pneumonia is not given antibiotics, or when a life-support machine is switched off, allowing someone in a long-term persistent vegetative state to die. This is called 'passive euthanasia' and is regarded as lawful and acceptable. Active euthanasia takes place when someone is given death-inducing treatment of some kind.

There is, in fact, no moral difference between the two kinds of euthanasia, because deliberately not doing something is as much an act as doing something. The concept in theological ethics of 'sins of commission and omission' embodies a recognition that equal responsibility attaches to deliberate withholdings and choices not to act, just as it does to failing to act when action is required. In that central respect passive and active euthanasia are the same. They both involve deliberate choices, and they both have the same outcome.

It is a matter of sentiment that passive euthanasia seems more acceptable. This point is more obvious when one recognises how often active euthanasia is in fact performed. Failure to shorten the suffering of a patient in agonising or terrifying terminal phases of an illness is so cruel that, in reality, few medical practitioners allow themselves to stand aside. To do so would be to treat people with less consideration than is typically accorded to animals, for we regard it as a kindness to animals to end their lives swiftly and easily when their suffering is otherwise unrelievable. But happily for human victims of pain or distress, in hospitals all over the world, every day, doses of painkillers are raised to fatal levels when needed, the legitimacy of the exercise protected by the 'doctrine of double effect', which says that because the doctor's primary aim is to alleviate suffering, the life-shortening side-effect is inescapable and therefore acceptable.

But as with the distinction between passive and active euthanasia, this is a conceptual convenience. Stating that one's intention is to relieve pain rather than to hasten death in such cases is a conceptual sleight of hand, given the empirical certitude that the latter will result. In any case, hastening death is the ultimate form of pain relief, and is therefore comprehended in the treatment to relieve suffering.

In discussions of physician-assisted death, whether direct in the sense of passive and active euthanasia, or brought about by 'double effect', the point is frequently made that medical practitioners are bound by their professional code of ethics to seek to save, protect, and promote life, or at least to minimise the suffering incident on accident or disease. In the United States appeal is still made to the clause in the Hippocratic oath which states, 'To please no one will I prescribe a deadly drug, or give advice which may cause my patient's death.' The principal meaning of this is that the practitioner vows not to bow to (say) family, political, or other kinds of third-party pressure to end the life of someone who does not wish to die. But some translations bear a reading that says the practitioner will not accede to a patient's request for death either, and this is the form of reading appealed to by opponents of medically assisted suicide. But clearly, a practitioner who refused to help a patient die who was in great pain, unrelievable and interminable (other than by death), would be failing in his Hippocratic duty to succour the patient; so the appropriate reading of the relevant clause in the oath is arguably the third-party one alone.

Nevertheless, there is a real concern for medical practitioners, whose primary *raison d'être* is to save life, ameliorate suffering, and to cure ills and injuries. For this reason a practical or institutional innovation might be suggested. This is that there should be a medical speciality of thanatology (I here coin a word from the Greek *thanatos*, death), that thanatologists should work within a careful framework of law and under the supervision of a hospital ethics committee, so that every occasion of thanatological treatment is approved in advance, monitored during administration, and properly recorded afterwards. Since only thanatologists will be involved in the work of helping sufferers to die who have elected such treatment and show a stable and intelligent intention to carry their wishes through, all other medical practitioners will continue to work under the assumption that their sole concern is to save life, cure ills, and palliate suffering. Apart from anything else, this will clarify the very grey area in which many medical practitioners now work, given the frequency with which they knowingly, and for compassionate reasons, administer life-shortening treatments.

Consider how the debate about 'the right to die' has evolved in the light of difficult cases in recent years, cases which have made the right, claimed by some terminally ill sufferers and others who wish to be in control of how and when they die, seem so hard to refuse. In some countries a 'right to die' is recognised, but not in many. In these latter the reasons usually given are practical ones, namely, the unwillingness of medical practitioners to kill when, as noted, their whole ethos is to cure or palliate; or the risk of abuses and murder under the guise of mercy, and the like. In countries where the right to die comprehends a right to physician assistance in doing so, the reasons are typically ones of principle; namely, recognition of the autonomy of individuals, which means their freedom to make choices about the character and quality of the ending of their lives.

The idea that individuals do not have this right – that, in other words, they are heteronymous with respect to their lives and bodies – is a central feature of Judaeo-Christian ethics. A god gave life, only a god can take it away; it is a sin to end one's life at a time and in a manner of one's choosing, for it usurps the prerogatives of deities in the matter. The secular principle of personal autonomy is in direct competition with such a view, and stands at the core of some key human rights ideas.

Inspecting how this is so brings out the point that each of the human rights standardly listed in human rights conventions requires to be explicated in a rich philosophical and jurisprudential debate in order to bring out its implications and sometimes concealed depths. The question of the right to die provides a focal example. Consider the thought that the right to life, the right to protection from inhumane treatment, the right to privacy, and the right to freedom of thought and belief between them entail that individuals have the right to die when and how they choose, with the further implication that they thus have a right to medical assistance to do so. One thought is that if an individual is denied the chance to die before his sufferings become intolerable, he would thereby be subject to inhumane treatment. Another thought is that the rights to privacy and freedom of belief constitute a right to self-determination – that is, autonomy – and therefore people have the right to decide what to do with their own lives, subject to the provision that they do no harm to others in exercising their rights.

I argue that a right to life itself includes a right to die. In a famous case that came before the English courts, the highest appeal court in the land – the House of Lords – came to the conclusion that the right to life does not embody a right to die on the grounds (so the judgment stated) that 'Death is the antithesis of life.' This is a crucial error. One must distinguish between the *state of death* and *act of dying*, and recognise that dying is a living process, something that happens while one is alive, when all one's rights are or should be fully engaged. It is easy to see why people are distracted from this realisation because the debate is about the manner, timing and circumstances of a process of dying. But consider: someone might be dying, and recover; one cannot claim that his entitlement to have his human rights respected diminishes or fades as his vital functions reduce, only to strengthen again as medical interventions bring him back towards health. It can be granted that once an individual is dead only residual rights remain in respect to him, for example as to his testamentary wishes.

Employing this distinction between death as a state and dying as an act helps one to spot the errors that follow from not observing it. First, although death is of course the antithesis of life, dying is not. As an act of living, dying is one of life's most significant events, which can be pleasant or otherwise, tragic or desired, timely or untimely. As any of these things it is integral to the experienced quality of an individual's existence. Death is not anything we experience; it is non-existence, a state (if 'state' is the right word) indistinguishable from being unborn. But unless one is unconscious while dying, the process of doing so is a fact of experience. And in the same way that we hope most of our living acts will be pleasant, we hope that the act of dying will be likewise – or at least not painful, frightening or undignified.

An allied point is that the word 'life' in 'the right to life' cannot denote merely basic existence. It has to mean life which has a minimum quality and value for the person living it. Along with the other rights standardly listed, it has to mean a life protected from the arbitrary abuse of power, in which the individual is at liberty to seek fulfilment among the opportunities that life normally affords, and which is free from excessive distress and suffering. These protections exist to ensure that no one can get away with saying someone's right to life is being respected if he is fed on bread and water in a cage. The life in 'the right to life' is life of a certain minimum standard in quality and opportunity; and what this implies for the ending of life is surely obvious.

As all this implies, mere existence, even human mere existence, is not an automatic good. Thinking otherwise would mean that life-support machines in hospital would never be switched off, even out of kindness; it would mean that contraception would be outlawed as an obstacle to the sheer accumulation of human numbers – a view taken by the Roman Catholic Church (while paradoxically encouraging abstinence and praising virginity). So there are those who oppose contraception and euthanasia exactly on the grounds that the generation and continuation of life are, respectively, such important matters as never to be trumped by considerations of its quality.

It takes little to see how questionable this view is. Placing the quantity of life at the same or a higher level of importance than its quality is misguided. Yet it is always questions of the quality of experience that figure in abortion – elected because of the consequences for the mother's life of proceeding to term – and euthanasia – the suffering of the individual who would quite literally be better off dead, and in the kind of case under discussion yearns to be so.

An oddity of the House of Lords judgment mentioned is that it made the assumption, or at least very much appeared to, that death is an evil. Most ordinary healthy people think, naturally and rightly, that they would like their deaths to be put off for as long as possible, because naturally and rightly they wish to continue to enjoy their relationships and avocations, and to realise their hopes. But for those who suffer, death is not an evil but a kindness. The point is sometimes made that we appear to be gentler to our pets than our fellow humans, for we put them easily and swiftly to sleep when their suffering is unrelievable, and yet we leave our human loved ones to linger and expire by the forces of nature, often in great discomfort.

At the other end of life, in connection with the question of abortion, matters are complicated by our instinctive tenderness towards babies. 'Pro-life' campaigners make frank use of emotive appeals in describing abortion as slaughter of the innocent. The truth is that abortion is always difficult and unpleasant, for it does indeed involve the ending of a form of human life. But this fact does not make it invariably wrong. There are many difficult things we have to do that are necessary or justified – in the name of compassion too, for a foetus always competes with established human interests and goals. Cases of deformed foetuses or endangered mothers seem most clear. Cases of (for example) pregnant schoolgirls seem more difficult; but here the rule should surely be to protect the actual commitments and projects of a present person, in balance with which the multiplying cells within her at most represent a potentiality. Of course this does not make the potentiality null; we accord rights of a kind even to the not-yet-conceived when we give future generations a claim on us to protect the environment in their interest. So *a fortiori* the conceived have claims too. This means that abortion can never be taken lightly, as when it is used for tidying up irresponsibilities in contraception.

But rather few women take abortion lightly, and many are hurt by the experience; yet most of them maintain, on sober reflection, that in the circumstances they made the right choice between continuing their lives as then situated, or undergoing the dramatic alteration that parenthood involves – even when the child is adopted, for the psychological burden of that can be very great.

Opposition to abortion is not exclusively religious, but

religion is one of its chief sources. Life is regarded as sacred because given by a deity, so ending it is a sin. This view does not allow that to create a lifetime of suffering is a far greater sin, as it is – say – to require a woman already overburdened with caring for other children to add to their number. It is not the sanctity of life (whatever that means, for it is not invoked in the conservative view on capital punishment and legitimate war) but the quality of life that really matters; and this last figures centrally among the justifications for abortion.

One way to think through the dilemma that abortion poses is to take seriously the idea, already premised, that it involves a conflict of interests (and a peculiarly difficult one). On one side there are the serious occurrent interests of an existing adult or near-adult individual woman with commitments, plans, circumstances, needs and constraints which affect the question of whether she is in a position to continue her unwanted or inopportune pregnancy, and raise the resulting child or give it away for adoption. On the other side is a developing foetus, at that stage strictly a set of potentialities as a future human individual. Of course both mother and foetus have rights to the protection and consideration of their interests, but the key is whether those rights are equal. Reflection on the contrast just drawn strongly suggests that the mother's interests so far outweigh those of the foetus that her right to have them protected must carry the day when they compete.

To repeat: there is nothing happy about the difficulty people find themselves in when such cases arise. Nature is profligate with foetuses, spontaneously aborting the great majority of them very early in pregnancies; and yet in some cases it is miserly with them, in the case of women who long for a baby but cannot conceive. It is hard indeed for these latter to look with equanimity on the tens of thousands of abortions performed voluntarily every year. But the best lights even of such a woman would enable her to recognise the possibility of lifelong tragedies for two people, and usually more than two, when there is no recourse for terminating unwanted pregnancies in a world of many burdens and difficulties.

CHAPTER 10

Religion and Reason

Because so much of the moral outlook labelled 'conservative' in preceding sections has its root in religious traditions, a comment on them is appropriate. There are no doubt sincere believers who find solace and inspiration in their faith and who do good because of it. To them the spectacle of religion's terrible record of bloodshed, cruelty and intolerance – throughout history, and still in this present day – must be painful. But the foundations of religious belief do not rely upon rationality for their acceptance; so it is not surprising that faith visits violence upon its heretics and opponents, for its roots lie in emotion – in hope, fear, subjective feelings of certainty, and psychological needs of various kinds. Those roots lie also in ignorance; religion began as the science and technology of earliest man, who, surrounded by fearsome nature, devised explanations of the universe ('It was made by an agency like us, only invisible and much stronger'), and a means of controlling (by prayer and sacrifice) its phenomena – especially the weather, the fecundity of herds, and the growth of crops, all so vital to life. The moralities that exist to ease human relationships came to be enshrined as divine commands, disobedience to which was seen as a threat to the precarious abeyance of storm and earthquake, drought and starvation, which, as divine anger, always impended.

Thus the first sources of much contemporary moral conservatism. But religion is in fact either irrelevant to questions of morality, or it is positively immoral. This claim undoubtedly seems contradictory at first, but a little reflection shows otherwise.

In an individualistic society, where personal wealth is the chief if not the sole measure of achievement, a morality that tells you to give away all your possessions to the poor, which instructs you to take no thought for the morrow ('Consider the lilies of the field'), that says it is easier for a camel to go through a needle's eye than for the rich to enter heaven, that preaches selflessness towards your neighbour and complete obedience to a deity – such a morality contrasts very sharply with the norms and practices not just accepted but extolled in Western society, where we are asked to be responsible for ourselves and our families, to plan and save, and to regard possession of the amenities and comforts of life (in other words: material things) as commendable. Most people therefore simply ignore the stark contrast between such views and today's manner of living, and pursue the latter. In this way religious morality is an irrelevance.

But when fundamentalists deny education and health care to women, practise genital mutilation, amputate limbs as a punishment, stone adulterers to death, murder those they oppose, extol suicide bombing and acts of terrorism in the name of their faiths, religion becomes positively immoral.

Much religious energy is devoted to controlling our sexual behaviour, either by disallowing it (or thoughts or representations of it) other than in strictly limited circumstances, or by preventing the amelioration of its consequences once it has happened. Thus, the righteous write complaining letters about televised nudity, while automatic rifles, handguns, shells, cluster bombs and rock launchers are exported from the factory next door to their homes to regions of the world gripped by poverty and civil war. With such examples and contrasts, religion has little to offer moral debate.

Some think that a deity is required to provide grounds for morality: 'Such and such is good (or bad) because God says so.' But as Bertrand Russell succinctly argued, 'Theologians have always taught that God's decrees are good, and that this is not a mere tautology: it follows that goodness is logically independent of God's decrees.' It might be added that if the will of a deity is the ground of morality, one's reason for being moral is merely prudential; it consists in a desire to escape punishment. But this, though sensible enough, is hardly a satisfactory basis for the ethical life – and threats are never logically compelling premises for any argument.

Consider one of the major religions most familiar to us: Christianity. It is an oriental superstition whose irruption into the classical world eventually overwhelmed the latter and changed the course of its development. It is fruitless to speculate how the history of the West might have proceeded if Christianity had expired, after a short time, as merely another version of various common and ancient Middle Eastern mythic themes, in which a god makes a mortal woman pregnant who then gives birth to a hero who attains heaven after mighty or miraculous deeds (think of Zeus' many mortal paramours and their offspring, such, indeed, as Hercules), the dying and reviving god as in Egypt or the myth of Persephone in the underworld, and so endlessly on. But we can make a guess, as follows.

For one thing, Plato's and Aristotle's academies in Athens would not have been suppressed in AD 529 on the ground of their 'pagan' teachings. The irony attaching to this occurrence is that their suppressor, Justinian, was the builder of the Church of the Holy Wisdom in Constantinople. For another, there would have been no Christians to put a stop to the Olympic games in AD 393 because of their dislike of athletes' nudity.

Apologists might say that without the accident of Christianity becoming the official religion of the Roman Empire, we would be without the glorious *Annunciations* and *Madonnas* of Renaissance art. But in balance with the sanguinary character of much Christian history – its crusades, inquisitions, religious wars, drowned witches, centuries of oppression – this seems a debatable loss. In place of *Annunciations* we would have more *Apollos Pursuing Daphnes*, more *Deaths of Procris*, more *Dianas Bathing*. By almost any standards, apart from the macabre and gloomy ones of Puritan sensibility, an Aphrodite emerging from the Paphian foam is an infinitely more life-enhancing image than a Deposition from the Cross.

The religious attitude is odd. It appoints certain writings as holy, and thereafter refuses to take seriously what they say. Consider this passage from the Book of Samuel – in its King James robes, a delightful piece of prose – and ask whether, if what it reports is exemplary of holiness, it inspires us to emulation:

> Then said Samuel, 'Bring ye hither to me Agag, King of the Amalekites.' And Agag came to him delicately. And Agag said, 'Surely the bitterness of death is passed.' And Samuel said, 'As thy sword hath made women childless, so shall thy mother be childless among women.' And Samuel hewed Agag in pieces before the Lord in Gilgal.

If the mincing of Agag wrought divine pleasure, then it is surely the Prometheus of Goethe who has the gods' measure: 'I know nothing more wretched under the sun than you, ye gods! Scantily you feed your majesty on sacrifices and the breath of prayer; and you would starve if beggars and children were not hopeful fools.'

Leslie Stephen pointed out that while religion flourishes, the only ethical enquiry that there can be is casuistry, the science of interpreting divine commands. The ultimate justification of these rests on a logical fallacy with a forbidding Latin name, the *argumentum ad baculum*, which means the threat of force.

The religious reply to the moral sceptic's question 'Why should I behave in such and such a way?' is simply, 'Because God requires it of you.' This is a polite way of saying, 'Because you'll burn if you do not.' The *argumentum ad baculum*, as a threat of punishment, is not a logical justification for acting one way rather than another. If there exists a deity with the punitive vengefulness of the Judaeo-Christian or Islamic God, then it might be prudent to obey it, and thus avoid burning; but the threat of burning is not otherwise a valid reason for obedience.

Religious apologists claim that our motive for acting morally should not be the threat of divine punishment, but love of God and our fellow men. But this is camouflage, however well meaning. For in the religious view, if someone chooses not to act on the prompting of such affections, or fails to feel them at all, he is not therefore excused exile in the place of punishment. He will meet the fate of the fig tree, which, we are told in a pre-environmentally sensitive biblical text, was blasted for bearing no fruit out of season.

If love (in the sense of *agape*; in Latin, *caritas*, hence charity) is the reason for being moral, what relevance does the existence of a deity have? Why can we not be prompted to the ethical life by our own charitable feelings? The existence of a god adds nothing to our moral situation, other than an invisible policeman who sees what we do (even in the dark), and a threat of post-mortem terrors if we misbehave. Such additions are hardly an enrichment of the moral life, since the underpinning they offer consists of fear, threats of violence, and endless sufferings, which is exactly what, among other things, the moral life seeks to free us from. Such threats precisely characterise the state of man under religion for most of history, which is why one can expect no better of religious morality.

Before the scientific revolution of the seventeenth century, humanity found its picture of the world a satisfying one. The world existed to serve mankind; it had been created by the deity for that express purpose. Our home the earth hung from the glittering floor of Heaven like a jewel, with Hell beneath and Chaos around; while above, in the crystal spheres, burned the greater and lesser lights, set in everlasting motion by the creator to illuminate our days and mark our seasons, making music, as they flew, too beautiful for us to hear while imprisoned in our 'muddy vesture of decay'. When it was proposed (by Copernicus, and empirically demonstrated by Galileo's telescope) that the earth flies too, and as one modest member of a vast swarm, occupying an insignificant corner of a vaster universe, the affront to human self-importance was incalculable. But the calm deductions and patient observations of science, not to say the extraordinary difference it has made to the condition of ordinary life, did not make opposition to science plausible for long.

Indeed, Galileo's story is a microcosm of the epic struggle between science and religion. Galileo was inquisitive, inventive, mathematically adept. He was fascinated by the view above him in the clear Italian night sky. He perfected the telescope, and used it to terrify the Church by revealing more stars than had been guessed before, hitherto unseen satellites orbiting other planets, and valleys and mountains on the surface of earth's own moon.

Because scripture taught that the earth stands still at the

centre of the universe, whose celestial spheres are driven round by angels, the Church could not tolerate this new vertiginous cosmology. The immovability of the earth, placed by the deity at the centre of a universe especially made for man, was explicit in the Bible: Psalm 102 says, 'He fixed the foundations of the earth that it shall not be moved forever.' Saying that the earth moves not only gave the lie to scripture, but thereby threatened the Church's authority. By the time-honoured expedient of threats and intimidation, Pope Urban VIII forced Galileo to recant his espousal of the Copernican system. The Church itself recanted this act only in 1992, two and a half centuries later; a length of time that speaks volumes about the conflict of faith and reason.

Such is one example of very many that could be adduced of the world-view and the mindset that underlies religious ethics. A non-religious ethics – let us, for convenience, give it the broad label of 'humanism' – is very different.

I use the term 'humanism' to denote an ethical outlook that is explicitly non-religiously based, resting instead on our best understanding of human nature and the human condition. At very least a humanist outlook aspires to premise respect and sympathy, and wherever possible liking, for fellow human beings everywhere. Others might do or be things that lose the respect of their fellow human beings, and there is no call even on a deeply ethical humanist to like violent people, fanatics, murderers, exploiters, despoilers and destroyers. But even so a humanist should be one who recognises that the forces shaping people's lives are complex, largely arising from the interaction between human nature's biological and evolutionary basis, and the particular social and historical circumstances that make each individual what he or she is. Understanding these things comes through appreciation of the arts, literature, history, philosophy, science, and through personal experience too.

All this adds up to the great conversation of mankind, one of whose central purposes is to help us – if we are attentive listeners – to live good lives, to do good to others, and to contribute some moiety of our individual gifts to building just and decent societies.

And all this is for the sake of life in this world, not for some suppositious other world. Much of the individual and communal endeavour of people serious about the good has of course to be directed at mitigating the bad sides of things that humans are and do – the unkind, angry, hostile, selfish, greedy, cruel, superstitious, ignorant sides. Knowing about these sides is part of knowing about the good, because the good is their opposite; and knowing what it takes to foster the good is part of recognising the work of the bad in the world – and why it is bad.

For a long time, and still in the minds of many, the quarrel between the good and the bad can be properly understood only in the Manichaean terms of religious morality, and it can only be answered by it. Reflection suggests otherwise. If it were argued that religions set moral examples unparalleled by secular outlooks such as political movements, the claim would be easily refuted. As noted, religions fare no better than most secular outlooks, including Nazism and Stalinism, which emulate religions in being monolithic ideologies demanding absolute subservience to a supposed ideal, on pain of death for disobedience; and they fare much worse than some – humanism, for example, has killed no one for disagreeing with it; there have been few wars fought over disputes in botany; historians do not stockpile anti-tank weapons for use against one another, except figuratively.

One might quote, 'By their fruits ye shall know them': one of the chief threats posed by religious militants is their use of the concept of blasphemy, even to the extent of justifying murder – a shocking reminder of earlier and viler times was forced on Western consciousness by the Salman Rushdie affair, and it is now alas a commonplace of our world again, most especially when any inflammation of (in particular Muslim) sensitivities occurs.

Etymologically 'blasphemy' derives from the two Greek words, *blaptein* and *pheme*, respectively meaning 'to injure' and 'reputation'. It could be, and has been, used to refer to imputation against the reputation of non-divine persons and institutions, but its primary meaning is of course 'any word of malediction, reproach or contumely pronounced against God', as the *Catholic Dictionary* informs us. That is an interesting definition, given that reproaches against the deity must be a daily commonplace in the sufferings of mankind, whether or not there has been a tsunami or a cancer diagnosis, a plague or ('Where was God in Auschwitz?') any of the horrors visited by humans on other humans because of the religious commitment of one side or the other.

If I reject or scorn your gods, in your view I blaspheme. If a missionary of a non-Christian faith visits a Christian country and tells its citizens that their belief in virgin birth, miracles and resurrection is false and perhaps even pernicious (as Christian missionaries told potential converts abroad was the case with their native faiths), and that they should instead worship his own deities, he would be branded a blasphemer. The alien missionary, of course, began this by laying the charge against his answering accusers, and would doubtless repeat it. And so the exchange would continue, until either he or they ended as cinders at some convenient stake.

Blasphemy comes into existence when someone's utterances offend others' religious sensitivities, the offence consisting in a perceived insult to something regarded as sacred or divine. But it depends on cases; and it always takes two – a giver and a receiver of offence – to make blasphemy possible. It is, in essentials, a product of conflicts between perceptions. The perceptions are subjective, shaped by tradition and often associated with cultural identity.

Because what counts as blasphemous depends so heavily on relativities and (non-rational) subjective commitments of faith, blasphemy is not an appropriate matter for law. Blasphemy laws, like those relating to obscenity and censorship, are instruments for controlling ideas; which implies, if anything, that blasphemy is healthy because it is an expression of free speech, and demonstrates the maturing of an intellectual community from one historical stage of belief and practice to another.

And yet, of course, aspersions real or perceived on what a given group regards as sacred have been, and in many places remain, subject to law, and often harsh law. Pakistan's current laws decree the death penalty for 'defiling the holy Qur'an' and making 'derogatory remarks about the Prophet'. Compare this to now-repealed nineteenth-century laws in certain states of the United States, where the penalty for anyone who

> wilfully blasphemes the holy name of God by denying, cursing or contumeliously reproaching God, His creation, government or final judging of the world, or by cursing or contumeliously reproaching Jesus Christ or the Holy Ghost, or by cursing or contumeliously reproaching or exposing to contempt and ridicule, the holy word of God contained in the holy scriptures

was anything up to a year in jail and a fine not exceeding $300 (this example is provided by Massachusetts).

But technically Christian punishment for blasphemy should be as Pakistan's is; Leviticus 24: 16 says that the blasphemer is to be put to death, and Luke 12: 10 says that blaspheming against the Holy Spirit is unforgivable – a dire saying indeed – supported by Mark 3: 29 where such blasphemy is deemed an 'eternal sin'.

The first and most obvious thing to be said about blasphemy laws is that they violate the most fundamental of all civil liberties, namely, freedom of speech. Without free speech all other civil liberties and political rights are empty. There cannot be democracy without free exchange of information and vigorous debate, involving challenge and criticism. There cannot be due process at law unless people can speak freely in accusing others or defending themselves. There cannot be proper education unless people can ask, answer, propose and criticise freely. Literature and the arts would be sterile. In short, without freedom of speech only a grey, duplicitous, failing, fearful and stagnant society such as prevailed in Soviet Bloc countries would be possible. It is no accident that the freeing of minds and speech in the sixteenth and seventeenth centuries AD in Europe, at great risk and cost, its advocates in danger of murder by the Church for heresy and blasphemy, is what made the modern world possible.

No system of religious ethics adds up to much, when dispassionately considered. Christianity is jejune in its principles. Nietzsche pointed out that the Beatitudes, saying that the poor, the meek, and the downtrodden are blessed and will receive a reward in an afterlife, bespeak the psychology of an enslaved people – he meant the Jewish experience of exile in Egypt before Moses – and he might have added that they have served the purposes of the comfortably placed throughout history, since they reconcile the poor and humble to their lot, and have long helped to prevent uprisings.

What little Christianity offers by way of positive moral

injunctions is indistinguishable from the Judaism that preceded it, or from Mohism in ancient China with its ethic of brotherly love and its concern for widows, orphans and social justice. But neither the Judaeo-Christian nor the Mohist ethics compare to the richness and insight of 'pagan' Greek ethics, or to present-day concerns about human rights and animal rights, which are much broader, more inclusive, and more sensitive than anything envisaged in religious morality. Moreover, concern for the welfare and rights of people, animals and the environment motivated by a sense of the intrinsic worth of these things, and not by divine threats and promises, is the only true source of morality.

This last point is a clincher. Religious ethics is based on a sanction of posthumous rewards and punishments. It makes goodness the diktat of a supernatural being. You do good, by the lights of your religion, in order to achieve eternal bliss. If there are indeed supernatural powers in the universe, it might be prudent to do what they require, whether for good or ill, in the interests of saving your neck; but even when the requirement is to do good, this motivation is not a moral but a self-regarding and self-interested one. If I see two men do good, one because he wishes to escape punishment by a supposed supernatural agency and the other because he respects his fellow man, I honour the latter infinitely more.

PART III

Society

CHAPTER 11

Civility and Civil Society

It was claimed above that the real question for anyone who – figuratively speaking – steps into Hercules' sandals at the moment of choice is not one of morality but of ethics: a question of how to live flourishingly as a whole person, and in ways that respect the choices of others and their differences from oneself. To consider this point, a different angle of approach is required, one that takes into account the medium in which ethical lives can be lived: the medium of an ethical society.

Consider the following thought. Despite much opinion to the contrary, the Western world is not currently entering a new immoral age; rather, it is suffering from a different phenomenon, namely, a loss of civility. Western societies in the twenty-first century are by many measures actually better, in 'moral' respects, than they were a hundred or so years earlier: compare Victorian London's child prostitutes, and ubiquitous and violent street muggers, to the situation today. Rather, what has happened is a partial breakdown of the tolerance and respect that allows space and opportunity in a complex pluralistic society for individuals to choose their own way.

This is an important point. Civility is a matter of attitudes and practices that give us ways to treat each other with consideration, thus facilitating our interactions. Youths spitting and swearing on buses offer merely superficial symptoms of the loss of civility and good manners; more serious are such things as the deficit of tolerance, the persistence of racism, the collapse of restraint at the margins of society. If anything, although our age is a moralistic one, it is not an age comfortable with itself, for it suffers a diminution of social cohesion. The obvious consequence is division and conflict.

Of course, civility, in its standard manifestation of politeness, can be a mask; it has always been open to abuse, and if people relearned their manners it would continue so; but that does not diminish the good that real civility does. It helps foster a society that behaves well towards itself, whose members take seriously the intrinsic value of others and the rights of those who are different from themselves.

The point of civil society is best understood by contrasting it with a situation in which there are deliberately no institutions for governing relations between individuals and groups: namely, anarchy, defined as an absence of structures maintaining a social and legal order, by compulsory means if necessary. One might, in brief and collectively, call such structures the 'state'. On a typical anarchist view, the state is to be replaced by a network of voluntary associations, unconstrained and unregulated by anything beyond goodwill between individuals.

The central weakness in the anarchist view is that individuals are to some degree self-interested, and not all self-interest is indefensible or irrational. The same applies to groups, such as families or tribes. Sympathies are limited, and so are resources; competition between individuals and groups is therefore inevitable. Competition can, and often does, lead to conflict. So unless there are rules to ensure fair competition and a just resolution of conflicts, the strong will trample the weak and injustice will prevail.

The anarchist's belief that people can live in unregulated mutual harmony is touching but naive. To his inadequate moral psychology he adds pieties about 'freedom' as the aim of the anarchic dispensation; but he fails to see that freedoms worth having require protection because of their vulnerability, and that it is precisely in pursuit of genuine liberties that people congregate into civil society and agree rules. The anarchist's mistake is to think that because tyranny is hateful the state should be abolished. A more rational idea is to abolish not the state but tyranny, by making the state fairer and freer, thus protecting its members from the depredations of the greedy and the vile, who are too numerous among us to make anarchy even a remotely serious option.

This is not to say that the liberal civil polity just envisaged is easy to devise or to run, because the very reasons that make it desirable also threaten its existence. Such a society is by definition pluralist, and pluralism means the coexistence of often irreconcilable and conflicting values. We might believe or hope that such can be resolved by the exercise of reasoned tolerance, thus achieving harmony. But conflict and the damage that results from it are almost certainly unavoidable.

Enlightenment thinkers believed that, by the use of reason, mankind can identify universal goals for itself, and both discover and apply the means of achieving them. They believed that science and rationality can overcome superstition, despotism, inequality and war. This faith was strongly opposed by critics who argued that different peoples have different needs and aims, and that there are no universal standards of reason and therefore no ultimate solutions for the dilemmas faced by humanity. If one accepted this latter opinion, one would have to accept that a liberal society is only one form of human possibility, with no special status vis-à-vis others; whereas what our earlier thoughts suggested was that such a society provides the best opportunity for the ethical life.

Here therefore one has to take a stand (as with human rights) and argue that although conflicts and difficulties are endemic to the human condition, it remains worth while quietly to push the claims of reasoned tolerance as a means of solving or at least managing them. Even if the critics of Enlightenment values are right – even if the relativist view that certain values are mutually irreconcilable is true, and even if there is no clear answer to the question of how a given present dilemma should be resolved – still we can say that tolerance and reason are our best hopes for maintaining the subtle and constantly renegotiated equilibrium upon which the existence of civil society depends.

To achieve a civil society, as the appropriate medium of ethical life, requires liberal education. By 'liberal education' I mean one that includes literature, history and appreciation of the arts, and gives them equal weight with scientific and practical subjects. Scientific literacy is an especially important component of liberal education; whether or not children continue to study a science subject at the highest levels of their schooling, they should still be taking regular classes in scientific literacy, so that they can be informed contributors to public decisions about what effects science and technology should and should not have on their lives.

Education in the arts and humanities opens the possibility for people to be more thoughtful as well as more knowledgeable, especially about the diversity of human experience and sentiment, as it exists now and here, as well as in the past and elsewhere. That makes people better able to appreciate the interests of others, so that they can treat them with respect, sympathy, and generosity, however different the choices those others make, and however different the factors that have influenced their lives. When respect and sympathy are mutual, the result is that the differences which can prompt friction, and perhaps even war, come to be bridged or at very least tolerated. Toleration is more than enough in a world otherwise threatened by oppositions that too often turn into murder.

The picture just painted is admittedly utopian; there were, no doubt, SS officers who read Goethe and listened to Beethoven on the record player before setting off to work in the death camps; so education even of the acculturating and liberal kind just mooted does not automatically result in better people. But it does so far more often than the stupidity and selfishness that arise from lack of knowledge and impoverishment of insight.

Liberal education in this sense is no longer regarded as an ideal in the contemporary West, most notably in its English-speaking regions. As mentioned in order to be regretted above, education is too much restricted to the young, and it is in any case a far less ambitious kind of education, geared too exclusively to the specific aim of gaining employment after school. This is unquestionably a loss; for the aim of liberal education is to produce people who wish to continue learning after formal education is over; who are reflective, and questioning, and know how to find answers when they need them. This is especially important in connection with the ever-present and often-recurring moral and political dilemmas of society, which have to be renegotiated every time they present themselves. In a good society, its members are equal to that challenge because they are informed and capable.

Really good education is expensive, and if a society is going to provide it as a common good and as a means of creating equality of opportunity, it requires major investment. But achieving the aim of universal high-quality education offers very great rewards. It would produce a larger proportion of people who are more than mere infantry in the economic battle, by helping them both to get and to give more in their social and cultural experience, to have more fulfilling lives both in work and outside it – especially in the pleasures of social intercourse, and in the responsibilities of civic and political engagement. People who think and are well informed are more likely to be considerate in every sense of this term than those who are – and who are allowed to remain – ignorant, narrow-minded, selfish and *uncivil* in the regrettable sense at issue here.

One thing that such a society needs to be is, as the foregoing implies, an equitable one, in which the distribution of social benefits reflects the worth of individuals' contributions. In Western society the head of a large corporation earns the same in a year as dozens of nurses between them do. It is possible that this situation is consistent with the idea of a good and just society, where the climate of expectations about relationships between people results in recognition of genuine merit, mutual respect for rights, and willing fulfilment of obligations. But it does not give confidence that Western societies are such societies; if anything, the prevailing trends of inequity and imbalance push in the opposite direction.

The aim of ethics, one remembers, is to identify conceptions of lives worth living – whole lives, well lived, satisfying and rounded. This needs the right setting: a society that tolerates diversity, allows opportunities, agrees – in a rational, generous, and enlightened manner – where the limits are, but nevertheless is just (fair, equitable), and so structured that it gives people genuine chances to make good lives for themselves. It is hopelessly utopian to expect that, even if an ideal society came into existence, all those living in it would be transformed. The workings of social institutions cannot replace the ethical endeavours that individuals have to make on their own account; indeed, by making choices and controlling activities on behalf of its members, a society negates the very basis of ethics; the great tyrannies of recent history demonstrate this point with painful clarity. But in fostering a climate of aspiration towards ethical goals, a society can produce a current in the general drift which draws along some of those afloat in it. It can educate and encourage; and where what it encourages is the willed insistence on values of reason, tolerance, and fulfilment, it offers a beacon to some, and a standard for all.

Among the many things people need for their well-being, apart from sustenance, shelter, and the social affections, is a sense of place in the world – an understanding, however tenuous and general, of what it is to be human, of what is distinctive about human existence, and of what humans can therefore expect and hope from life. This philosophical need is not often recognised for what it is, but most people find a way of satisfying it. They usually do so by means of religion, either in the form of one of the traditional theistic faiths or – in the individualistic West especially – a mix-and-match version of the more comforting and less demanding aspects of them. But increasingly it is a much more modern outlook that provides their answers, namely, scientism, the belief that one day soon science will explain everything about the world and what it contains, including ourselves. The marvellous achievements of science (and its horrendous mis-application to the technology of war) are not at issue here; they are unquestionable. But scientism deserves a warning note, as promising false routes to human self-understanding and flourishing.

With the dramatic increase in knowledge and power provided by science, and in particular the biological sciences and computing technology, scientism has grown in influence. It goes further than the justified admiration that any reflective person must feel in contemplating science's great beauty and efficacy, because it believes that everything in the universe, including the subtle and ambiguous realities of human subjectivity, will one day be reduced to the language of biology and perhaps finally, when it has reached its perfected state, to the language of physics. This applies not just to what happens inside the skin of an individual person, but to the culture and society he inhabits.

As one would expect, opponents of scientism argue vigorously that this view is mistaken and meretricious. Science's success in explaining nature has made its more ardent votaries think it can therefore explain human nature. Darwin's theories have proved immensely powerful in unlocking the secrets of life's history, and have therefore given rise to the belief that human nature can likewise be understood in evolutionary terms; a prime example is evolutionary psychology, which says that all aspects of human behaviour, together with the cultures and societies it variously prompts, is explicable by reference to the features of human nature that were laid down in mankind's early evolution. But this essentialist view wholly ignores facts about the intricate interplay between human subjectivity and culture which no mechanistic account can hope to capture, and it gave rise to horrors – racism and the Holocaust among them – in its profoundly misguided application in the realm of politics.

As evolutionary biology prompted a reduction of humanness to the non-human animal realm, so developments in

computer technology and cognitive science prompted reduction of mind – the rich array of conscious and subjective
phenomena that make up a human being's mental life – to
mechanism: the mechanism of computational devices, on
the model of computers but embodied in the 'wetware' of
the brain rather than the 'hardware' of silicon chips. One
answer to both reductions is to insist on the exceptional
character of human subjectivity, and with it the culture and
society it produces, and to argue that nothing in the concepts of science is capable of explaining these more protean
phenomena. Because they lie outside science's domain they
have to be understood in different terms – as a shorthand for
which some reclaim the label 'humanism'. Although some
feel the temptations, this need not be an argument in defence of religion, or mysticism, or ignorance, but can serve
instead as a case for saying that human reality is *sui generis*
and invites humanistic approaches requiring concepts and a
vocabulary distinctively its own.

According to some commentators, it is an oddity of the
current situation that people fear what genetic science might
do, and yet crave evolutionary explanations of how nature
has formed us. The fear stems from the sense that science
'disturbs our moral compass', as one commentator put it,
by upsetting traditional ideas of human nature and destiny.
Troubled by moral disorientation and uncertainty, people
ycarn for myths to explain humanity's place in nature – and
sometimes they yearn also to be relieved of responsibility for
humanity's future and well-being. On this view, scientism
replaces deity with nature itself, which is why people turn
to nature for answers to dilemmas and reassurance about
the future. But this rearrangement also makes us pessimistic
about ourselves, because naturalistic accounts of humanity
make it seem the victim of deterministic causal processes
– our aggression, our gender differences, even the diseases

we might suffer and die from, are somehow ineluctably coded into us, a new version of the ancient Greek concept of inexorable fate. Biologists themselves are quick to point out that such views are mistaken; genes are not determiners but incliners. But social theorists, economists and others do not often enough heed their caveats. And it is this that critics of scientism object to; for them, 'emancipation from nature is essential to moral progress'; to free ourselves from tyrannies of all kinds, we need to be freed especially from the tyranny of nature. And one principal way of gaining that freedom is to see that human subjectivity and culture is not explicable in biological terms alone. We need history, philosophy, literature and the arts too. Understanding this is a prerequisite for understanding human interests and entitlements.

And obviously enough, one primary locus of explanation is the system of values which has evolved to provide a setting for thinking about moral progress and identity. A classic contemporary account of the political values at issue is provided by Ronald Dworkin, in a discussion that seeks to reconcile the fundamental principles of liberty, equality and community which many commentators have seen as mutually inconsistent, and yet all of which are required for workable systems of human rights.

Dworkin argues that the three virtues at stake – liberty, equality and community – are not, as so many theorists of both left and right have argued, incompatible, but instead are complementary aspects of a single vision, in which each depends for its realisation upon the existence of the others. That vision animated the awakening comities of Eastern Europe and parts of Asia, and it was what animated the revolutionary ardours of the eighteenth century. But each of the three has to be properly understood in its own right if we are to see how they reinforce one another, which is a task Dworkin set himself in focusing principally on the concept of equality, currently the least fashionable of the three ideals, and perhaps the most endangered of all species among political concepts.

It is endangered because, whereas centre and left politicians of the mid-twentieth century would have been unanimous in claiming that the formation of an egalitarian society is their ultimate goal, that aspiration is no longer part of the left–liberal vocabulary. Such politicians came to speak of a 'third way' instead, to distance themselves both from the right's abandonment of individuals to the harsh operations of the market, and from the 'old left's' belief that all citizens should share equally in their nation's wealth. But Dworkin pointed out that the now-rejected concept of equality was never a sustainable one anyway. It was that every member of society should have the same share of society's wealth as anyone else, irrespective of whether they merited it; as Dworkin remarked, such equality cannot be a value because 'There is nothing to be said for a society in which those who choose leisure, although they could work, are regaled with the produce of the industrious.'

Instead, Dworkin argued, equality must be understood in terms of the equal concern for its citizens that any legitimate government must show – 'Equal concern is the sovereign virtue of political community: without it government is only tyranny' – and equality of resources or opportunities, giving everyone a fair start in making something of their lives. The two equalities are linked; a government which shows equal concern for all its citizens would work to minimise the kind of disparities in ownership of resources, or access to them, that give some people an unfair initial advantage over others.

To the ideal of equality of resources Dworkin added that of personal responsibility for making good use of them to create a flourishing life. Each individual has a special responsibility for his or her own life, so even though society has to regard each individual as being equally important in the scheme of things, it cannot be expected to take the place of the individual himself (other things being equal) in the management of his life. Here is where liberty enters, not in conflict with equality as Dworkin defined it, but as part of it, because liberty is as essential a component of equality as equality is essential for the existence of liberty.

A significant feature of the arguments Dworkin deployed is their engagement with – and opposition to – two other famous and influential contemporary views: the value pluralism of Isaiah Berlin, and the liberalism of John Rawls. Berlin believed that liberty and equality are unresolvably in conflict, and that liberal society consists in the constant uneasy negotiation between them. Rawls attempted to base liberalism on the idea of a social contract, allowing questions of political morality to be separated from more general ethical considerations, not least from controversies about the nature of the good life. But in common with all those who have thought in the tradition of the classical philosophers – and especially Aristotle – about the connection between social and individual concerns, Dworkin insisted on holding that political values are seamlessly part of larger ethical considerations, precisely the premise of the view here taken about human rights. And this view is all the more discussible because turning attention to human rights is to turn attention to the prospect of a global ethics, and therefore of something even more inclusive than the idea of a good society: the idea of a good world.

CHAPTER 12

Human Rights and Universal Ethics

The Greeks used their tales of gods and heroes to explore aspects of morality and psychology because such tales allow for generalisation. A fable can apply to many experiences that merely resemble them in overall contour, whereas actual historical episodes have too many specifics to make them applicable to lots of different cases that are merely similar. Hence the power of legends, tales, myths, and stories. In the case of Hercules, whose labours took him across the known world and even out of it, the tale has a prescient universality about it; it is a morality play for all humankind.

In the eighteenth-century Enlightenment the same universalising spirit returned to a secular, this-worldly application in thought about the rights and liberties of individuals. The Herculean task that the thinkers of the Enlightenment set themselves was to persuade mankind that all individuals, no matter who, where, when, and what they were, possessed rights just in virtue of being human, which if respected would open the possibility for them to make good lives for themselves if they chose.

There is nothing abstract about an interest in human rights. Any witness to the need for them can tell stories about individual cases which, in their way, can be more telling than generalities, except of the most egregious kinds; just consider the examples of the Holocaust of European Jewry, Stalinism, Pol Pot – it is needless to list them. By themselves they make the case for the central importance of human rights – or should.

But in the quiet recesses of the academic study there are those, seeking reputation not in the cannon's mouth but in contrariness, who write entire books on the subject of human rights putatively to show that the idea of them is at least flawed, at worst bogus. One criticism targets the universality of human rights concepts, arguing instead the relativist line that different traditions, cultures, creeds and ethnicities have different and, on their own terms, equally valid conceptions of rights and entitlements at variance with the Western view.

Another and allied criticism is that judgements about what counts as a right – indeed judgements about all moral and morality-relevant questions – are subjective, and cannot be held valid across differences of subjectivity.

A third criticism exploits the argument made famous by David Hume, that descriptions of how things are in the world – in this case, specifically how they are with human beings – can never by themselves entail any moral judgement; one cannot derive an 'ought' from an 'is'. The effort to do so is labelled 'the naturalistic fallacy'. Yet (continues the objection) this is what all talk of human rights does, for it describes certain situations (say, a group of men applying red-hot pincers to another man's body in order to encourage him to supply them with information) and claims that this ought not to happen.

Another objection has longer roots. It is that implicit in the idea of rights is the claim that they belong inherently to human individuals just in virtue of their being such. But two centuries ago Jeremy Bentham and Edmund Burke both argued that there is no such thing as an inherent right, on the grounds that rights are accorded either by decisions of governments or by tradition, and do not mysteriously arise out of the nature of humanity itself.

Some critics also say that claims about rights are arbitrary; we decide that this or that is to be a right, and we dress it up in the language of 'inalienability', or we tacitly or otherwise try to give talk of rights a theological basis ('All men are created equal').

All these arguments are eminently refutable, and if one thought that a genteel debate about the matter could proceed while real people are being tortured, while genocides occur, while most people around the world lack the liberties, amenities and safeguards that most of the critics of human rights themselves take for granted, one would be happy to offer such refutations point by point. But another reaction, the one which for brevity might as well be adopted here, is to leave them to their dissertations, and to turn to the real questions. Suffice it to say that no normally constituted person could regard the claim that the description 'a group of men applying red-hot pincers to another man's body in order to encourage him to supply them with information' entails nothing as to the goodness or badness of what is happening. Subjectivists, relativists, and those persuaded by the naturalistic fallacy argument, oppose this; though it is interesting to speculate whether they would persist in doing so if red-hot pincers were being applied to their own bodies.

One can short-cut all such debates by agreeing, in part, that we arrogate rights – that is, we choose to constitute certain desirable states of affairs as being rights to which human individuals, just in virtue of being such, are entitled. But doing this is not a merely arbitrary move. All our experience of what conduces to good – all our insight into what limits human possibility, causes suffering, and is felt as cruel and unjust by victims; all our understanding of what we wish for ourselves, at the minimum, in the way of treatment by others and the institutions we live under; all our best, most sober, most mature, most well-judging debate among ourselves – teaches us what is both desirable and needful in the way of ethical and legal frameworks for the best kinds of human life. To rebut this manoeuvre, subjectivists and relativists have to say that it is not a general truth about human beings that they generally wish to stay alive, to enter into relationships with others, to eat, to be sheltered from the elements, and to have chances of making a life for themselves that they feel is good. That is tantamount to saying that although we do not wish to be murdered, starved, frozen or tortured, others might not share this outlook. Such critics can hardly be taken seriously.

Here is a personal detour into the question of motivation for asserting the importance of human rights to the world. I spent most of my childhood in central and east Africa, during the period of British government of the territories abutting the Congo and along the southernmost end of the Great African Rift Valley. They were British territories, 'protectorates', not colonies in the sense that expatriates went there to settle as they did in Kenya and what was then called Rhodesia. Later, upon gaining independence, the two territories respectively became Zambia and Malawi. When I lived there the populations of those countries were governed, policed and organised by my fellow British who came to mine copper or grow tobacco and tea. Native Zambians and Malawians worked as labourers or domestic servants on pittance wages, and occupied crowded 'compounds' or 'locations' on the outskirts of towns where we, their white masters, lived in considerable comfort.

My family occupied a large, cool, dim colonial bungalow with high ceilings and a fly-screened veranda all round it, in a garden with a tennis court and swimming pool and groves of tropical fruit trees – mango, avocado pear, pawpaw, passion fruit, banana palms. In one corner of the grounds, beyond the garages, stood a row of concrete huts secreted behind a wall, with a small adjacent plot for maize planting. This was the 'compound', the quarters set aside for the servants and their families, who between them made a numerous assembly. The cook and house-boys worked a six-and-a-half-day week, the gardeners a five-day week. Their wives and children had to keep out of sight and sound; my mother, the iron-fisted matriarch of the establishment, brooked no disturbance to her repose. When television first came to this remote African interior, consisting of a single channel that ran for four hours every evening, the window of the drawing room would fill with a couple of dozen silent faces peering in from outside to see the marvel of the flickering screen.

I soon enough grasped the inequity, not to say iniquity, of this situation, and it made an early and enduring impression. It was radically deepened by the experience of visiting the Republic of South Africa two thousand miles to the south, then still in the grip of apartheid. The obsequious and cringing attitude of 'non-whites' to their white overlords, which I instantly recognised as half satire, half necessity, was a shock. Buses and park benches, beaches, public lavatories, indeed the entire world was divided into two zones marked by signs proclaiming 'Whites Only' and 'Non-Whites Only'. It seems scarcely credible now: 'Whites Only'! (I remember a variant, in the form of signs saying 'Europeans Only'.) And everything for 'Whites Only' was superior in every respect to what was for 'Non-Whites Only'. Everywhere that non-whites went they had to have a 'pass book', a passport to navigate the streets of their own home towns.

It is hard to understand, but a grateful fact nevertheless, why those who had been subjected to this regime of discrimination, humiliation and diminution of their humanity, their subjection to poverty, to worse than second-class status, to contempt on the grounds of their skin colour alone, did not rise up when freed at last, and take sanguinary revenge on those who had done this to them. It does them extraordinary credit that they did not. One of the greatest examples of humanity to be drawn from the twentieth century is Nelson Mandela, without whose example and force of personality these matters might have been different. He gives the lie to Tolstoy's view that individuals make no difference to history, by demonstrating the truth that there is such a thing as individual moral heroism.

The white man in Africa: what a chapter in human affairs, beginning with slavery centuries ago and advancing – scarcely the right word – to conquest and exploitation. In the Americas the white man enslaved, exterminated, and dispossessed by the million in order to take possession of those continents and their wealth. The story is made no better by having been repeated so often. The quest for wealth, which is the lifeblood of power, reached its long iron tentacles out of Europe and crushed what it met, and we live with the consequences now. For me the matter is not personal in the sense that I was one of the victims of the process; but it is personal in that I witnessed it from the exploiters' side of the moral divide – involuntarily, as a child, but soon conscious of being allied to wrong.

Much later I came to have an involvement with China, first by living and teaching there and then visiting often to lecture and travel, and to write two books about it with co-authors. When the events of spring and summer 1989 occurred – culminating in tanks rolling over bodies in Tian An Men Square under Chairman Mao's watchful portrait

HUMAN RIGHTS AND UNIVERSAL ETHICS 153

above the Forbidden City's gates – being a bystander was no longer an option. For a decade afterwards I worked with, and for a time chaired, a human rights group working on China and its dissidents and asylum seekers, lobbying at the Commission and Sub-Commission on Human Rights in Geneva every year – an education in itself about the wider world of human rights, or more accurately: wrongs – briefing British government officials, organising human rights events elsewhere, including Hong Kong before its hand-back to Chinese sovereignty, and more. Focusing a beam of light on one spot somehow lights up the whole surrounding field; from Tibet to the Indians of the Amazonian basin, from asylum seekers in Britain to genocide victims in Rwanda, from the plight of women everywhere in the Third World to their especial plight in Taliban Afghanistan: the injustice and suffering in the world becomes deafening the moment one listens to one voice raised in despair.

To repeat: I was not a victim, but a witness – but then so are we all – disturbed and moved by the plight of people I knew. Theory is scarcely to the point here; talk of human rights is serious talk, because violations of them are serious matters. It is about real people and their real agonies of mind and body. And the fact that there are human rights organisations that lobby, complain, inform, campaign, demand and accuse, has palpable effects: individual lives have been saved, prisoners freed, regimes shamed, sanctions imposed, differences for the good made – even if patchily, even if in too few cases and too infrequently, against too great a backdrop of indifference or inaction by those who should know better and can do better – which is to say, governments.

In truth, these are early days in the great project of trying to make the whole world a place where human rights are fully respected. In the early phases of the twenty-first century, distracted by problems of religious resurgence and the conflicts it fuels, many seemed to think that the aspiration for human rights dimmed rather than brightened. But the idea of globally applicable human rights is still very young; the mechanism of enforcement of them is younger still. The International Criminal Court (ICC) is far more recent, and yet only feeling its way as an instrument for enforcing human rights provisions by bringing people to book for violating them. The ICC had many sceptics before it even came into existence, and many sceptics remain. What is the alternative? The near-anarchy that prevails in too much of international affairs, an anarchy that frequently – one can say, regularly – spills over into wars?

Almost all of these matters discussed in the foregoing have as their focus the ethics of individual life. But – to repeat, and the point bears endless iteration – human beings are social animals. This crucial fact was central to the question of relationship raised earlier, specifically, the relationships that an individual has with other individuals and his or her close community. The more general question of whether there is an ethics available to the community of humankind in general still presses. In response, the suggestion is that concepts of human rights provide a basis for exactly such a thing: a framework for a global ethics. But it also needs to be said that the generalities and benevolences of the great human rights proclamations, especially the United Nations Declaration of Human Rights (UNDHR), have to be fleshed out with vigorous and detailed debate about all that they mean; and that is a task humanity would do well to set itself straight away, now that the world is fully globalised and the frictions along the borders of cultures and traditions are all too obvious to see.

The hope is that general global agreement about a framework of values will make individual good lives possible everywhere. Again, to say so is admittedly utopian – but the opposite is to abandon ourselves to something like a pessimistic fatalism, having it that many and perhaps most lives will never be optimal, but almost certainly bad in many respects.

Contrast the sentiment in the Preamble to the UNDHR, which states, 'Recognition of the inherent dignity and of the equal and inalienable rights of all members of the human family is the foundation of freedom, justice and peace in the world.' Although inspection shows this to be a very large claim – not least in respect of peace – it also shows it to be true. For if a state contemplated making war on another state, and (*per impossibile*) paused to think about the inalienable rights of the non-combatant citizens of the putative enemy state, they would not – if they were fully seized of the import of the UNDHR's Preamble – because they could not, carry through with their first intention. This is pie in the sky of course, in the unhappy state of things in the world as at present constituted; but the aspiration is there, and it is at least imaginable that one day everyone will think it unimaginable that these words should be publicly known without being universally acted upon.

There is a deep resonance in the words 'inherent dignity and equal and inalienable rights of all members of the human family'. Speaking of rights Thomas Paine said, 'Man did not enter into society to become worse than he was before, nor to have fewer rights than he had before, but to have those rights better secured.' He was writing in the period when the first claims to a full set of individual human rights, in the sense of that expression now familiar, were made by the first nations to do so (the American and the French). In thus instituting a framework of rights as a bastion for the individual, the Enlightenment revolutionaries – and revolutionaries they truly were – were not appealing to something inscribed in statues or a golden age, but were starting afresh from a rational perception of what is minimally required for the human good. They knew their Cicero: 'The fundamental principles of justice should not be deduced from a praetor's proclamation, as some now assert, nor from the tables of the law, as our forefathers held, but from the innermost depths of philosophy,' and the Enlightenment agreed.

What are human rights? What is their basis? Are they universal or culturally determined? Are they a Western idea imposed on the rest of the global community? The answers to these questions are more than merely important, because they underlie the hope that human rights concepts can serve as the basis of a universally acceptable system of values, whose purpose is nothing less than that of steadying relationships in a divided and often dangerous world. The task – one is inclined to say, the responsibility – is to argue that concepts of human rights can and must command agreement across cultures and traditions, and thus provide standards of life for individuals, criteria of responsibility for governments, and a framework for international law. There is something profoundly noble about the hope.

Concepts of human rights are of course ideals, and great difficulty attaches to realising them in practice. But that is no reason to resist what for increasingly many is a passionately held conviction: that the development of human rights thinking, and especially human rights laws and institutions, is one of the most significant advances ever made in human ethics. Here I sample some of the considerations that should arise in more detailed discussion about the way that the idea of human rights can and should serve as the basis for a universal ethics.

*

Man's inhumanity is a tragic commonplace of human history. But in the twentieth century the technology was available for this inhumanity to be expressed on scales and in ways hitherto scarcely imaginable. The difference was one of degree, not kind; if Genghis Khan and Shaka the Zulu had possessed machine-guns, bomber aircraft, Zyklon B, or any of the other appurtenances of organised modern mass murder, they would assuredly have used them. It is the tragedy of our time that technological development has so far outrun moral development.

Yet the experience of war in 1914–18, and especially the crimes committed by Nazism in the period between 1933 and 1945, made for a vastly greater urgency in thinking about how to apply ideas about rights in practice. Specifically legal conceptions of 'crimes against humanity' and 'genocide' had to be fashioned almost from scratch for the Nuremberg trials; these ideas, together with the debate during and immediately after the war about human rights, constituted marks of hope in the midst of chaos and slaughter.

People who think that the modern age is wickeder than earlier times are inclined to blame the fact on a weakening of moral sensibility, which they in turn blame on the waning of religious belief. Some regret the diminution of religion's influence not because they are themselves committed to the tenets of one or another faith, but because they think that a certain moral climate is fostered by the existence of a strong religious presence in community affairs. This consideration still weighs with those, whether secular or not in other respects, who think that faith-based schools will, say, improve child discipline and self-restraint.

On the basis of what was said above about the relation of religion to morality, it is not needful to explain again how traditional religious moralities do not help matters by themselves, for morality has to be grounded and justified independently of the metaphysical claims about the existence of supernatural agencies and their demands on their creatures. Rather, moral ideas have their life in application to human beings in social settings. That is the point insisted upon and iterated in all the enlightenments of the Western tradition from classical antiquity to the age of science.

The implicit neutrality in the human rights focus on questions of morality means that, as the fundamental ideas required for agreement across cultures and creeds, concepts of human rights have to have, as an aspect, an openness to what else people might add to their moral outlook that does not conflict with human rights principles. In almost all human rights conventions the right to freedom of conscience and belief is accordingly enshrined. The problem – one to be resolved – is that some of these superadded belief systems directly conflict with others of the rights in those conventions; and that is a problem that the contemporary world is having laboriously and painfully to engage with yet again. A chief example is the position of women in traditionalist Islam.

Given that concepts of human rights offer a framework for ethics grounded on facts about human needs and interests, and given that these potentially conflicting discourses seek to cut across the grain of those needs and interests, the matter is a serious one. I characterise this opposition, for convenience, as the tension (and often worse) between the new framework and traditional frameworks – but remember that the new framework would accommodate the traditional frameworks subject to the latter making themselves consistent with it – and consider (in the next chapter) some ways in which the cost of the new framework being undermined by the traditional frameworks would be too high.

CHAPTER 13

Wars and Their Crimes

One such way is to reflect on the efforts made in discussion about, and applications of, human rights doctrines in the period since the Universal Declaration of Human Rights was adopted in 1948, together with the eventual setting up of the International Criminal Court as an instrument of enforcement of the international legal regime to which the Declaration of Human Rights and its two great Conventions (respectively on civil and political rights and on social and economic rights) have given rise. The establishment of the International Criminal Court in particular was motivated by the determination of supporters of the new framework to bring an end to genocide and other crimes against humanity, and to do so by having effective remedies against those individuals and groups responsible for human rights violations.

One arena where these ideas are becoming more influential is that of war, in particular in connection with the idea of 'just war'. The phrase looks like an oxymoron, given the murderous and destructive nature of war at its poor best. And that thought is a good one. But at the same time the obdurate fact is that wars happen, and that the struggle to minimise the harms they do is therefore a necessary struggle.

Acceptance of the fact that engaging in war is on occasions

justified, though war is ghastly however viewed, is demonstrated by the Allied case for fighting Nazi Germany and Japan between 1939 and 1945. Interesting and persuasive hindsight cases can be made for saying that all-out war might have been avoided if the international community had taken strong and decisive collective action much earlier than 1939, but it did not do so, so there was war, and the question is whether the Allies were justified in going to war. On the merits, the answer is an emphatic yes. Matters having got as far as they had, the Second World War was, from the Allies' perspective, a legitimate use of arms to defend against and to defeat aggression, and to bring an end to tyranny and genocide.

Just war theory derives mainly from St Thomas Aquinas, who in the second part of his *Summa Theologiae* rebutted the proposition 'that it is always sinful to wage war' by arguing that a war is just in circumstances where three conditions are met. These are, first, that there is a just cause for the war; second, that it is begun on proper authority; and third, that it is conducted with the right intention, namely, that it aims at 'the advancement of good, or the avoidance of evil'.

Modern theorists have added two other conditions to Aquinas's three. One is that the war must have a reasonable chance of success, and the other is that the means employed in prosecuting the war must be proportional to the ends sought.

The first of these additions is a pragmatic one; a possible understanding of it is that a government commits an injustice against its own people if it takes them into a war that they are more likely than not to lose. In the light of the quixotic courage of, say, Polish lancers charging their horses towards German Panzers, thereby encouraging defiance and setting an example of resistance that helped, in its way, eventually to win the war, this prudential consideration scarcely seems fit to be counted a moral buttress in thinking about just war.

More controversial, as it has proved, is the second addition. War leaders as different as Winston Churchill and Mao Zedong iterated the point – which on the face of it seems obvious enough – that in fighting to the death one does not tie one hand behind one's back. Mao's chilling comment was, 'War is not crochet.' But do such opinions license the use of nuclear or chemical weapons, except perhaps *in extremis* when the alternative is annihilating defeat for one's own side? In this connection the just war debate extends into the question of just actions in war; supposing one had a just cause for going to war, might one not compromise one's moral standing in the case by acting unjustly in the employment of means to conduct it? The point need not be pushed so far; a war might be just from one point of view, and yet involve an unjust aspect, as with Allied area bombing of civilian populations in the Second World War.

Aquinas's three conditions are clear enough and persuasive enough in themselves to make the case for the claim that there can be such a thing as just war. The real question is whether they are genuinely met in any given case where they are alleged to be (most cases do not even merit the bother of discussing whether they do, for almost all war is unjust and illegitimate). One can always ask: are the circumstances of this case such that the principles apply? Was there really a just cause for going to war here? Are the avowed aims the true ones, and are they good?

There are clear examples of just causes for war. Defending against invasion or aggression is one; going to the aid of a threatened people is another. What about pre-emptive military action against a possible aggressor? History teaches the danger of appeasement and inaction – the Second World War again supplies a stark lesson – but can one ever be certain that an assessed threat is truly dangerous enough to go to war, and can one be certain that claiming to be threatened is not a disguise for aggressive ambitions on one's part?

Yet a people surely has the right to self-defence, and the best form of defence, it is said, is attack. Would that justify going to war? After all, a government fails its people if it does not prevent them from being assaulted by enemies.

Aquinas said that the aims of just war are promoting good or avoiding evil. Unless one has an inflated sense that one's self-interest is conterminous with 'the good' in the largest sense, it is ruled out as a just cause of war, along with need for *Lebensraum*, oil fields, or the enlargement of empire. 'Avoiding evil' can be claimed by those taking pre-emptive action; 'promoting good' would have a chance of being an acceptable motivation only if it issued in peace, stability, prosperity, and a situation in which both winners and losers could cease being enemies.

But even if we grant that the Aquinas conditions are clear and persuasive, they are arguably insufficient by themselves to justify going to war. Other factors merit consideration. Has diplomacy failed? Is there no alternative to the use of military force to achieve whatever (putatively good) aims are in view? In the pragmatics of international relations, diplomatic efforts and, when they fail, various forms of encouragement or pressure (the latter including economic sanctions) are the typical means for dealing with problems, making the military option a later if not a last resort. In fact on any view it is hard to describe a war as just if it is not the last resort in the case.

I repeat a point that seems to me the clincher: that a truly just war would be a war of ideas aimed at ending the rivalries, the differences of view, the misunderstandings and tensions that lie at the root of all human conflict. Winning such a war would make it possible for all swords to be turned into ploughshares at last.

It would be comedy if it were not tragedy: moral philosophers in ivory towers reacted to the twentieth century's atrocities by claiming that it was not their task to address the question of wrong, and to continue Socrates' debate about how people should live, but rather (they said) to examine the precise meanings of the terminology used in moral discourse, together with the logical relations between moral statements.

Those philosophers were in part right; there is indeed a job to be done of careful analysis of the concepts bandied about in moralizing, and of the kind of reasoning – practical reasoning – employed in speaking about what should and should not morally be done. There are brilliant insights in the technical and scholarly debate focused on these questions. Some of those who disclaimed the mantle of guide or guru did so for the admirable reason that, once the terms of moral discourse had been clarified or at least illuminated, it was up to everyone else to think for themselves on the basis of their understanding of them. And that too is right. What was lost, however, was the connection with the richly valuable tradition of meditation on the right and the good, initiated by Socrates and developed by his successors in the tradition of philosophy from the Stoics of the Hellenistic period to the Enlightenment so crucial to our own times.

Or rather, it seemed to be lost; for even while some of the most distinguished holders of philosophy professorships in the universities were making these disclaimers, around them was growing up a variety of discussions which have since come to be collected under the name of 'applied philosophy', chief among them medical ethics, business ethics, environmental ethics, and debates about animal rights.

These pursuits, with an avowedly practical bent, took their rise from the realisation that we need to reflect on how to live and choose in a world that is changing so fast and in such large ways that we are in danger of being overtaken by our own ingenuity – an ingenuity that outpaces the growth, if it can be called that in the face of contrary evidence, in the wisdom and maturity of our civilisation.

Medical ethics is a prime example of this important and necessary development. Until recently the only ethical rules that medical people explicitly acknowledged, apart from 'Do not advertise and do not have sex with your patients', consisted in a professional code originally suggested by the Hippocratic commitments to patient confidentiality, and to the aim of curing where possible but otherwise at least avoiding harm.

In this view, which might be called the Hippocratic ideal, the central and exclusive concern is the practitioner–patient relationship, and although medicine has changed out of recognition from Hippocrates' day, that is still the case. But the nature of the relationship has become a far more complex one. There is the matter of patients' rights, notably that of giving and withholding consent with regard to treatment; there is the closely related question of whether, and if so in what circumstances, paternalism is justified; there is the practitioner's duty to tell patients the truth; there is the question of how practitioners are to choose in cases of divided loyalties – as when considerations of public health are urgent, or when to ask a patient who satisfies the protocols for an important medical trial whether he or she would be willing to take part. This can be tricky if the patient is dangerously ill and the experimental treatment holds out some promise of a cure, yet some risk.

From the commencement of life to its end – from the technologies of reproductive treatments to abortion, from dilemmas over withholding treatment from severely deformed neonates to difficulties about the extent of medical intervention and life-support for elderly patients, and on to physician-assisted suicide and euthanasia – the ethical dilemmas posed by medical advances multiply and increase in urgency. We need to understand them, reflect on them – and always seek to do the generous and kindly thing. This reprises the points made about euthanasia and abortion earlier.

CHAPTER 14

Enforcing the Rights of Man

A thorough discussion of human rights as the basis for a universal ethics would have to address a set of familiar but complex questions, among them the problem of relativism and the history of non-Western traditions of social thought, the problem of religions and religious practices at odds with secular universalism – and the allied matter of inter-religious differences over rights. It therefore includes questions about women's rights, gay rights, minority rights, as well as the functioning, even the possibility, of the wholly general values of tolerance and liberty, plus the question of limits to the applicability of law to matters of private conscience.

It would also, as we have seen, have to ask the hard question of how human rights provision can be enforced, given that all the declarations and exhortations in the world will change little unless they are backed by remedies for those who have suffered, and sanctions for those who have caused them to suffer. This is where the idea of the ICC represents one major kind of hope for an order of things in which human rights ideas have concrete application.

Critics of the ICC dwell at length on the practical difficulty of making such a court work, and the related likelihood that its existence will reduce the United States' willingness to police the world. They base this criticism in important part on the belief that there is no such a thing as an 'international community', and that therefore only an historically evolved practice of law-governedness in tribal, ethnic, or national settings can work. And because there is no 'international community' the assumptions and hopes of human rights advocates are bound to fail, based as they are on what critics take to be the false idea that humankind can be holistically viewed as a nation or tribe writ large.

These critics also charge ICC advocates with seeking to 'subdue national sovereignty through the back door of international law', and they regard the ICC as undemocratic, believing therefore that it is not morally right that such a court should exist. The assumptions behind this view – that law works only on a national level; that only there can it be democratically accountable; that only there is it the result of the organic evolution that justifies it and makes it suitable to its domain – are important ones, and have to be addressed fully by any supporters of the idea that there should be international enforcement of human rights provisions.

Essential to the case for the ICC is the principle that mankind is a single big (though too often unhappy) family, and that it is a mistake to be committed to thinking that smaller units – the nation, the ethnic group – are the natural and proper basis for law and community.

First, we live now in a globalised and interdependent world. None but the least-developed sectors of undeveloped economies is free of international connections. This has been increasingly the case since 1945, and that is why there is now so much effective international law in the commercial and maritime domains. The ICC envisages a far more precisely defined role in the criminal sphere than these; the mere fact of their existence, and their utility, are therefore hopeful signs. Global interdependence, and the existence of hundreds of effective international institutions from charities like the Red Cross to UNICEF to the International Court of Justice in the Hague (to say nothing of large treaty organisations like trading blocs and multinational military alliances), show that supra-national groupings, and by extension the international community itself, are concrete realities. Critics of the ICC imply that the feebleness of the United Nations is evidence to the contrary; but although the UN is indeed paralysed by divisiveness among its members, and drastically hamstrung by lack of funds, it has not long been in existence – and global consciousness is growing fast, as proved by the very fact that the ICC itself exists.

Second, the nation-state in which some repose so much faith is an entity with a short and horribly troubled history. Whereas one can understand the concept of humankind (as contrasted, say, to chimpanzee-kind or rabbit-kind), the concepts of 'tribe', 'race', and 'nation' are peculiarly difficult to grasp and, if graspable, they are deeply unattractive. Their logical conclusion can be seen in Hitler, and the phrase 'national sovereignty' grates on the ear as *casus belli*, which it has far too often been. It is certainly a mistake to think that state boundaries, almost all drawn on the world map by wars, confer sacred status on the groups of people living within them. The notions smack of racism; nationalism (racism's disguised maiden aunt) is especially fruitful in generating conflicts, even though there is hardly any set of political boundaries anywhere that encloses a racially homogeneous people whose ancestors have tilled their land since Noah. If critics have a point in this connection, it concerns democracy; but the descendants of Germans in Pennsylvania, and Frenchmen in Louisiana, and Spaniards in California, and Englishmen and Dutchmen and Irishmen in New England, all have a vote in the same elections in a country as big as all the states of Europe together; so it would seem that large political entities of diverse peoples can be democratic, and one cannot think of any reason to put an upper limit on the numbers involved. (Perhaps critics will reply with another practical objection!)

In the past, slowness of communication made political units small. It took time and effort to introduce the rule of law over increasingly large communities, and there were many failures. Those who enjoy life in law-abiding communities do well to give thanks for that blessing daily. The ideal of bringing all humanity under a single rule of law, by consent and with mutual aid in making it effective, is admittedly utopian; but as with anything in which the principle is indisputably good, the task should be to strive to approximate it as closely as possible. That is what the ICC represents, and arguments to the effect that only nation-state institutions can work, and that there is no such thing as an international community (no such thing as mankind? no such thing as fellow human beings elsewhere in the world?), ring hollow in comparison.

CHAPTER 15

Back to Hercules

One of Hercules' tasks was fetching the Golden Apples of the Hesperides – a far western point in the mythical geography of the ancient mind – not because those legendary apples were made of gold, or because they were famous or desirable, but because they were distant and difficult to get. Hercules had to enlist the help of Atlas, who held the world on his shoulders, to secure them. The apples' remoteness was their very point, seen from the perspective of the fact that Hercules was under a necessity of accomplishing very difficult things in order to be free.

Does it seem that arguments about an International Criminal Court are a long way from, say, the note of beauty in the construction of lives felt to be good by those living them? Does it seem that discussion of human rights is as remote from discussion of the good as the Hesperides were remote from Hercules' Greece?

Perhaps the most significant thing one can say about the good life is that reflections respectively about the ICC and the note of beauty are far closer to one another, considered as contributing aspects of it, than at first appears. The connection lies in Aristotle's remark that ethics and politics are the same thing. It is hard (not impossible, but hard) for there be good individual lives in social arrangements that are bad, where people are oppressed, denied, deprived, limited, frustrated, coerced, and stunted. The worse the degree of these things, the harder it is for individuals to forge good lives. The real point of politics is to build circumstances in which good individual lives can flourish; that is a prescriptive point, not – as history, alas, shows – a descriptive one, for most political organisations have existed for the benefit of a few, or a class, and the idea of the welfare of all is a latecomer in the world. Even as such, it is often more lip-service than reality, though in Western democracies it has a certain bite, because the voting in and out of governments and presidents does have an effect, even if too often it is not as great as politically conscious and active citizens would like. The Herculean labour therefore falls as much on politicians earning re-election as on the active citizens – in the ideal, all citizens – charged with the final authority on what is done, and why.

The interesting point is that politics thus serves ethics; the point of making good societies and good communities is to make conditions right for there to be good individual lives. It ought to be clear from the foregoing that this is not an assertion of overweening individualism, nor a claim that the isolated human is the true unit on which good life is premised. The individual human unit is that premise, yes, but not the isolated human unit; to say so would be to miss the point about the note of intimacy and relationship made earlier, as applying to an essential fact about people: that we are social beings. Thus, politics is inescapable. But it is not the main point. Politicians fall into the trap of thinking that it is so, whence arise too many of our difficulties. But the focus remains with real people, individuals in relationships with each other, all seeking and meriting a chance to realise the good.

Under other names or none, consciously or not, that is

what all of us do. And since that is so, it is worth repeating – again and again – the point that the life best worth living is the informed life, the considered life, the responsible life, the chosen life, in which sound the notes that together, in harmony, make for fulfilment in the active sense of well-being and well-doing that Aristotle nominated as the mark of moral success. It might be a Herculean labour at times to achieve this success; but the choice any would-be Hercules of the good life should make, is at least to try: for it is the endeavour itself which is the greatest part of the good.

Acknowledgements

My thanks to Alan Samson and Francine Brody at Weidenfeld, to Catherine Clarke as always, to David Mitchell and Mick Gordon for inspiration and example, and to Rebecca Wilson, Florence Mackenzie, Sophie Erskine, and Naomi Goulder for help past and present.

Select Bibliography

Ackrill, J. L., *Aristotle the Philosopher* (Oxford, 1981)

Anderson-Gold, S., *Cosmopolitanism and Human Rights* (Chicago, 2001)

An-Na'im Abdullahi, Ahmed, *Human Rights in Cross-Cultural Perspective: A Quest for Consensus* (Philadelphia, 1992)

Aristotle, *The Complete Works*, ed. J. Barnes, 2 vols (Princeton, NJ, 1984)

Arnold, E. V., *Roman Stoicism* (Cambridge, 1911)

Austin, M. M., *The Hellenistic World* (Cambridge, 1981)

Bailey, C. M. A., *Epicurus: The Extant Remains* (Oxford, 1926)

Barnes, J., *Aristotle*, Past Masters series (Oxford, 1982)

Barnes, J., *Early Greek Philosophy* (Harmondsworth, 1987)

Berlin, Isaiah, *The Crooked Timber of Humanity* (London, 1990)

Boardman, J., Griffin, J., and Murray, O. (eds), *Oxford History of the Classical World* (Oxford, 1986)

Bouswsma, W. J. *The Culture of Renaissance Humanism* (Washington, 1973)

Bowra, C. M., *Homer* (London, 1972)

Campbell, T., Ewing, K. D., and Tomkins, A., *Sceptical Essays on Human Rights* (Oxford, 2001)

Camus, A., *The Myth of Sisyphus* (London, 1955)

Cicero, *On The Good Life* ('On Friendship', 'The Dream

of Scipio', and selections from 'Tusculum Discussions', 'On Duties', and 'The Orator') trans. Michael Grant (Harmondsworth, 1971)

Cochrane, C. N., *Christianity and Classical Culture* (Oxford, 1944)

Crawford, J., *The Rights of Peoples* (Oxford, 1992)

Crombie, I. M., *Plato: The Midwife's Apprentice* (London, 1964)

Davis, M. C., *Human Rights and Chinese Values* (Oxford, 1995)

Dawkins, Richard, *The God Delusion* (London, 2006)

Douzinas, C., *The End of Human Rights: Critical Legal Thought at the Fin-de-Siècle* (London, 2000)

Dunne, T., and Wheeler, N. J. (eds), *Human Rights in Global Politics* (New York, 1999)

Dworkin, Ronald, *Life's Dominion* (London, 1993)

Epictetus, *Discourses and Encheiridion*, 2 vols (Harvard, 1925)

Gearty, C., and Tomkins, A. (eds), *Understanding Human Rights* (London, 1996)

Gill, R. (ed.), *The Cambridge Companion to Christian Ethics* (Cambridge, 2000)

Grayling, A. C., *What is Good?* (London, 2003)

Grayling, A. C., *Among the Dead Cities: Was the Allied Bombing of Germany and Japan in World War II a Necessity or a Crime?* (London, 2006)

Grayling, A. C., *Against All Gods* (London, 2007)

Gruber, G. M. A., *Plato's Thought* (London, 1980)

Guthrie, W. K. C., *The Greeks and their Gods* (London, 1950)

Guthrie, W. K. C., *A History of Greek Philosophy*, 6 vols (Cambridge, 1962–81; 1962)

Hardie, W. F. R., *Aristotle's Ethical Theory*, 2nd edn (Oxford, 1980)

Harff, B., *Genocide and Human Rights: International Legal and Political Issues* (Boulder, Colorado, 1984)

Hart, H. L. A., *Law, Liberty and Morality* (London, 1966)

Hayden, P., *The Philosophy of Human Rights* (readings and documents) (New York, 2001)

Holloway, R., *Godless Morality* (Edinburgh, 1999)

Hsuing, J. C., *Human Rights in East Asia: A Cultural Perspective* (New York, 1985)

Hume, David, *An Enquiry Concerning the Principles of Morals* (Oxford, 1998)

Irwin, T. H., *Plato's Moral Theory* (Oxford, 1977)

Irwin, T. H., *Aristotle's First Principles* (Oxford, 1988)

Jones, G., *Social Darwinism and English Thought* (Brighton, 1980)

Kristeller, P. O., *Renaissance Thought* (New York, 1961)

Lauren, P. G. *The Evolution of International Human Rights* (Philadelphia, 1998)

Lear, J., *Aristotle: The Desire to Understand* (Cambridge, 1988)

Levi, P., *The Drowned and the Saved* (New York, 1989)

Levi, P., *Survival in Auschwitz* (New York, 1995)

Lloyd, G. E., *Aristotle: The Growth and Structure of his Thought* (Cambridge, 1968)

Lovejoy, A. O., *Essays in the History of Ideas* (Baltimore, 1948)

Lucretius, *On The Nature of Things* (Harvard, 1975)

MacIntyre, Alisdair, *After Virtue* (London, 1984)

Mackie, J. L., *Ethics: Inventing Right and Wrong* (Harmondsworth, 1977)

Marcus Aurelius, *Meditations* (London, 1992)

Mill, J. S., *On Liberty and Utilitarianism* (London, 1864)

Mill, J. S., *Three Essays on Religion* (London, 1874)

Mithcell, B. G., *Morality: Religious and Secular* (Oxford, 1980)

Nietzsche, F., *Beyond Good and Evil: Prelude to a Philosophy of the Future*, trans. and ed. Walter Kaufmann (New York, 1966)

Nietzsche, F., *On the Genealogy of Morals* and *Ecce Homo*, trans. and ed. Walter Kaufmann (New York, 1969)

Nietzsche, F., *The Twilight of the Idols* and *The Anti-Christ*, trans. R. J. Hollingdale (Harmondsworth, 1977)

Outka, G., and Reeder, J., *Religion and Morality* (London, 1973)

Persico, J., *Nuremberg* (New York, 1996)

Plato, *Collected Dialogues*, ed. E. Hamilton and H. Cairns (Princeton, NJ, 1961)

Pliny the Younger, *Letters* (Harmondsworth, 1990)

Plutarch, *Moralia* (Harvard, 1949)

Randall, J. H., *The Making of the Modern Mind* (Cambridge, Mass., 1940)

Renteln, A. D., *International Human Rights: Universalism versus Relativism* (The Hague, 1990)

Robertson, A. H., and Merrills, J. G. (eds), *Human Rights in the World* (Manchester, 1972; 4th edn, 1996)

Robertson, G., *Crimes Against Humanity* (London, 1990)

Russell, Bertrand, *Marriage and Morals* (London, 2005)

Russell, Bertrand, *The Conquest of Happiness* (London, 2006)

Sandbach, F. H., *The Stoics* (London, 1975)

Sartre, J. P., *Essays in Existentialism* (New York, 1993)

Seneca, *Letters* (Harvard, 1920)

Seneca, *Moral Essays* (Harvard, 1920)

Shue, H., *Basic Rights* (Princeton, 1996)

Shute, S., and Hurley, S. (eds), *On Human Right* (Amnesty Lectures, London, 1993)

Sieghart, P., *The Lawful Rights of Mankind* (London, 1985)

Singer, P., *Writings on an Ethical Life* (London, 2000)

Smith, P., *A History of Modern Culture*, vol. 2, *The*

Enlightenment (New York, 1934)

Venturi, F., *Utopia and Reform in the Enlightenment* (Cambridge, 1971)

Williams, B., *Morality* (Cambridge, 1972)

Williams, B., *Ethics and the Limits of Philosophy* (London, 1985)

Yolton, J. et al., *The Blackwell Companion to the Enlightenment* (Oxford, 1991)

Index